STAGE-SETTING

FOR AMATEURS AND PROFESSIONALS

STAGE-SETTING

For Amateurs and
Professionals

by

RICHARD
SOUTHERN

THEATRE ARTS BOOKS
NEW YORK

Printed in Great Britain

Library of Congress Catalog Card Number: 62-12339

CONTENTS

Preface to Second Edition   *page*   9

PRELIMINARIES
The Scope of the Book—The 'Costume' Setting and
the 'Symbol' Setting   13

CHAPTER ONE
BACKGROUND SETTING WITH NO PROSCENIUM

Section *1.* The 'First Piece of Scenery', an Introduction to Stage-carpentry   21

Section *2.* The Simple Side-hung Curtain   41
Section *3.* The Side-hung 'Arras' Setting—The Guy-
rope Set—The Birth of the Proscenium
Arch—An Introduction to Sight-lines   50
Section *4.* An Explanation of Stage Directions   60
Section *5.* Footed Screens—Folding Screens   64
Section *6.* The Lighting of Background Sets   76

CHAPTER TWO
THE PROSCENIUM COMES INTO THE STORY

Section *7.* The Fourth Wall—Curtain Fit-ups supplying their own Proscenium   81

Section *8.* The Construction of a Separate Proscenium
Arch — The Simplest Proscenium — A
Built-in Proscenium — A Temporary
Proscenium   90

Section *9.* The Etiquette of the Front Curtain   101
Section *10.* The Working of the Front Curtain   106

CONTENTS

CHAPTER THREE
PURE CURTAIN SETTINGS FOR THE PROSCENIUM
STAGE

Section 11. The Curtains   *page* 115

Section 12. The Battens and Lines for Hanging   121

Section 13. Openings and Backings   136

Section 14. The 'Armed-Batten' Curtain Set and the
'Rochdale Curtain Theatre' Set   142

CHAPTER FOUR
THEORETICAL INTERLUDE: A DISTINCTION
BETWEEN STAGE-SETTING AND SCENERY

Section 15. The Existence of a Distinction—Defini-
tions of Scenery, Setting, Details of
Scenery, Full Scenery, Permanent Set,
Standing Scene—Inconsistence of Cer-
tain Styles with Modern Art Theories—
An Analogy with Illustration   149

Section 16. The Inessentials of Scenery and the
Origins of a Mistake—The Rise of
Scenery—The Fortuitous Incidence of
Perspective—Realism   159

Section 17. The Parting of the Ways—(*a*) Detail
Setting, (*b*) Full-Theatre Procedure
with Full Scenery—The Limitations of
(*b*)—We return to examine (*a*)   165

CHAPTER FIVE
DETAIL SETTING

Section 18. Eight Varieties of Detail Setting: 1,
Painted Detail—2, Built Detail—3, Re-
presentational Built Detail—4, Real
Detail—5, Frame Detail—6, Selected
Real Details on Special Background—
7, Selected Real Details on Fantastic
Background—8, Screen or Skeleton
Detail   169

CONTENTS

Section 19. Details among the Curtains: The Use of Doors and Windows in Curtains—A Note on Painted Detail Construction, a Rough Method of Framing a Set-piece —Varieties of Painted Detail   *page* 175

Section 20. Details and Script, 1: An Introduction to the Scene-plot   190

Section 21. Details and Script, 2: The Birth of Three Specific Shows—1, *Abraham Lincoln*   195

Section 22. Details and Script, 3: Constructing the Details—Doors, Windows and Fire-places   207

Section 23. Details and Script, 4: Three Specific Shows —2, *The Green Goddess*—Plotting and Arranging—Construction of Set-pieces, Arch-pieces, Rostrums and Steps   219

Section 24. Details and Script, 5: Three Specific Shows —3, *Romeo and Juliet*   233

Section 25. A Simple Special Arrangement   244

Section 26. Finale—Standardization and Specification   248

Bibliography   260

Extension to Bibliography, 1937-1963   261

Footnote to Second Edition, 1964   262

Index   265

Preface to the Second Edition

The publishing date of the first edition of this book was 1937; since then a world war and over a quarter of a century have passed by. In 1937 it never occurred to me that the book might continue to be useful to readers for so long a time. I considered it then no more than a collection of notes on what I had to learn when I first went into stage setting as a job, and my intention was to supersede them at the first opportunity with more detailed notes of more elaborate methods, going eventually into full scenery.

I in fact took one step towards this original intention by publishing *Proscenium and Sight-lines* in 1939, which is a full guide to the dimensioning and planning of all types of scenery, both simple and elaborate, and I still use and am satisfied with the system it describes. But I saw that my further intention of recording the technique of more complicated scenery could be quite well served by simply adding certain new books to my original bibliography. Little had been written in any detail about the technicalities of full scenery when *Stage Setting* was first published but in the following years this gap began to be filled, and so the further projected books of mine became unnecessary. Thus it was that I turned from the study of scenery to a problem that was receiving far less attention at that time; the design of the stages on which the scenery had to go, and finally to the relation of the stage to the auditorium and the whole question of theatre architecture. But that is outside the scope of the present study. To bring my early intention up-to-date I have added an extension to the bibliography which the reader will find on pages 261 and 262. This will point him to all the later books with which he can continue into the deeper complexities of the subject of scenery.

9

All the same, despite the growth of more advanced information, the present book has still continued in demand, and about 1960 it found its way to readers across the Atlantic. I was interested to see that a reviewer there, about that time wrote of *Stage-Setting* ' . . . this book is a disappointment . . . it is a summary of many techniques for simplified staging, used by little theatres in this country since the early 1920's . . . And finally, the bibliography is unsatisfactory in that publication dates are often omitted, and where stated indicate that most of the books are old, having been published before 1934.' All perfectly just criticism—except that the reviewer did not apparently know that the book had in fact been written before 1937.

I felt that I must take some action about this misunderstanding. If, now, new American readers were to be added to the old long-standing line of English readers, then I ought to warn them they were buying an old book and must judge it as such—indeed as a piece of history, not a modern *reportage,* or at the best as *reportage* of ways practised a quarter of a century ago.

In addition to all the above came a warning that the current re-printing was nearly exhausted. Should we put out a further re-printing or go for a new edition? A completely new edition could get over all the difficulties.

But book production costs had rocketed in those many, often troubled years so that there was no prospect of producing a new edition at anything like the same cost as the old. To keep the price down there was only one recourse, and that was to reproduce the old edition as it was but with the addition of a foreword or a postscript.

And yet this seemed hopeless! How could a book as old as this, on a subject that had seen so vast a development, be re-issued unaltered and hope to escape the scathing critcism of 'out-of-date'?

I re-read the text grimly and began to make sheets of notes of what I would like to alter. But then I noticed something. What needed altering was chiefly the unimportant. Prices, proprietary names of goods and supplying firms had changed; but such things are in any case matters for local verification by any careful reader (especially if he is over on the other side of the Atlantic). And if I put them right for 1964, they might be still outdated by 1965. Furthermore, time had taken from us many of the persons mentioned. But their work remains and needs no change into the past tense (and in any case time continues to take persons in spite of new editions).

Supposing then that we might effect this particular modernization by a simple foreword asking readers in this second half of the century to treat commercial and personal references as historical by now—I went on to ask which of the ideas in the text stood in need of modification in the light of experience?

In general these were only ideas concerning historical usages—ideas about the methods of the past. Research into theatre history has developed astonishingly in the last two decades, and I would no longer consider the picture of an Elizabethan theatre as given on p. 55 correct in including such a hypothetical thing as an 'inner stage'. Richard Hosley's article on 'The Discovery-Space in Shakespeare's Globe' in *Shakespeare Survey* No. 12 (Cambridge 1959) well sets out the modern objection to this view. Also I would prefer today to see a *Romeo and Juliet* played on a stage of Elizabethan character rather than in the picture-frame manner described in Section 24 (p. 233)—but this is a matter of personal taste. Again I do not now remain happy with my views on the origin of the proscenium arch on p. 54. I think that what I have since said on the subject in *The Open Stage* (1953) p. 50 is closer to the truth.

(Also, reading at the middle of p. 59 I was reminded that Bertolt Brecht has shown that you *can* have a front curtain whose top isn't hidden!)

Further, with regard to the comment about the raked stage-floor on p. 62, I have learned how many dancers and some actors (for instance Sir Donald Wolfit) still strongly prefer a raked stage. Their views were summarized in an article in *Tabs*, vol. 14 no. 1 (p. 20) and no. 2 (p. 16), 1956.

Once more, I should like to add a footnote on p. 157 to the effect that you *can* today use a typical, traditional picture-frame stage without a full set of scenery to mask the 'ugly' walls; as John Bury well showed in his settings for Theatre Workshop at Stratford, E.—especially notably in Marlowe's *Edward II* in 1956.

A final small note in this department: I would change the words relating to two methods of presentation, 'the Elizabethan and the Jacobean', to 'the Elizabethan and the Restoration' on p. 159, 9 lines from the bottom. That was an error.

And lastly I come to the matters of fact contained in the book. It was on this score that I made my decision to agree to a second edition unaltered. There is little (I know what a bold thing this is to say!) to require changing here; it is all basic technique, and basic techniques survive. It is as useful knowledge for theatre in the round as for the traditional stage of the 'thirties. Indeed some of the technical methods in this book are *more* suitable now to modern experimental styles than they were to the orthodoxies of thirty years ago. I decided, then, to add a footnote on these matters at the end of the book and hand the 1937 text to the reader unchanged.

London 1964

PRELIMINARIES

The Scope of the Book—The 'Costume' Setting and the 'Symbol' Setting

This book is both a guide for the amateur stage-manager and set-designer and a record of professional procedure in a particular type of theatrical setting. The usual professional methods of to-day are here collected and described and certain extensions and modifications are outlined to suit the particular circumstances of amateur or improvised stages.

It is my hope that, firstly, the professional will welcome an effort to put a somewhat ill-defined and (save by stage-carpenters) a too-little understood technique in order upon paper so that he may use the result, if he wish, as a starting-point for fuller and more particular notes of his own; and secondly, that the amateur, realizing how desultory are the efforts either to use or study theatrical setting properly in his own field, will make this outline of professional procedure (addressed as it is so much to himself and his needs) a basis on which to broaden his tradition of setting his shows before his public.

For the purpose of study we may divide the whole subject of Theatrical Setting into eight varieties:

Simple Setting	1. Costume Setting. 2. Symbol Setting. 3. Background Setting. 4. Pure Curtain Setting. 5. Detail Setting.	Treated in detail in the present book.
Full Scenery	6. Wing-and-cloth Setting. 7. Box Setting. 8. Cyclorama Setting.	

This book is concerned only with the first five of these, which may be grouped together and, for our purpose, called the *simple* varieties, as opposed to the last three styles, that we will term *full scenery* and must leave for treatment elsewhere.

Of the five 'simple' styles, the first two we may dismiss in a moment with a single note. With the third, fourth and fifth, it is the purpose of this book to deal at length.

Even with these our main concern is with the use, construction and arrangement only, but the vital subject of *the design upon the scenery* it is more convenient to treat as a branch of scene-painting. For reasons of space I shall make no attempt in this book to touch any of the departments of scene-painting; that must come after a grounding in the technique of building, assembling and planning settings. This book is intended to supply a groundwork in so far as simple setting is concerned.

It will be convenient to divide our study here into three parts:

1. *Setting without a proscenium*, where we shall deal with Background Setting and the presentation of shows in the simplest halls or rooms, innocent of any special theatrical features such as a proscenium arch or devices for hanging scenery (Chap. 1).

2. *The building of a proscenium arch*, where we shall turn from setting for a moment in order to carry the simple platform of the first chapter a step forward, towards the characteristics of the ordinary theatre (Chap. 2).

3. *Setting in curtains with a proscenium*, where we shall return to setting and develop the methods of the first chapter so as to adapt them for the proscenium stage, and shall discuss both the Pure Curtain Setting and the Detail Setting, the latter forming one of the most flexible and useful methods of setting shows that can be found (Chaps. 3, 4 and 5).

At the beginning let us notice that a show can be presented without scenery or a theatre at all, just as were the earliest shows in history. The eight varieties at the beginning of this chapter form a sort of historical sequence, and there will be found in this book several references to the history of theatrical setting and to methods used in the past. No apology is made for this because no sure and intelligent knowledge of the job can be had without some acquaintance with its tradition and some understanding of the original meaning and the development of the items one uses.

The earliest way of all was to set the show merely with the costume and masks of the players.

Then came the second style, when, added to the players and their costumes, was some symbol—a ritual wand stuck in the ground (like the Maypole) or some such significant object—around which the presentation of the show was hung. That was the first scenery and its study is a very great help to understanding the function of a setting to-day.

Thereafter we come to shows presented in some sort of 'theatre', though possibly no more than a bare hall or a yard or a lawn, with or without a raised stage. Here we come upon the Background Setting, as I have called it, and the beginning of our study.

There follows the development of the hall into something more nearly resembling a theatre as we think of it, with the new-born proscenium arch. If in such surroundings we start again with separate objects like the symbols of old, simply details (though now perhaps of considerable elaboration) but now set against a special background, we have the style I name Detail Setting.

Beyond that we should come to full-theatre technique, where the whole of a fully equipped theatre stage is used and the various forms of Full Setting are practised—Wing-and-cloth Sets, Box Sets, Cyclorama Sets and Permanent Sets. This we must leave to another occasion.

To the Costume Set I shall give no more than this allusion, but of the second style, the Symbol Set, the following example may prove a useful introduction before we go on to begin our main story with a discussion of Background Sets.

Fig. 1 shows an example of the direct application of Symbol Setting to a modern college hall. The platform at the end of the hall was designed for the masters' use at prayers, and at either side carries tiers of curved benches. On the wall at the back, below the coloured-glass window, is the panelling of a roll-of-honour board whose presence we cannot conceal, so we must accept and thus forget it. The straight lines on the floor before the platform indicate the first rows of spectators' seats.

Fig. 1. A large school hall offering few facilities for a show and where no fixtures may be made.

It is required to present a version of *Thersytes*, a mediaeval 'interlude' of a comparatively riotous and satirical nature, taking place before the Smithy of Mulciber, Lord of all Blacksmiths.

No scenery can be achieved in the particular circumstances. Problem: how to set the show? It is a good example of the extreme problem as it presents itself to those attempting a show in unprepared or inadequately prepared places.

The stringency of the conditions simplifies the solution. There is no question, How are we going to hang the curtains? —because no curtains are to be used, nor, How can we adapt the set to the existing stage entrances?—because there is none. It is a case of absolute zero. So we resort to one of the oldest methods in the world.

Upon the rectangle you see drawn on the floor of the stage, a little to the side of centre, we erect a little 'tent'—a framework of poles covered loosely with blue casement cloth.

It is as yet a tent and nothing more. But if upon the small circle you see drawn beside it we stand an anvil, the tent is another thing; our anvil is an all-pervading symbol and our smithy is established.

In Fig. 2 you see our unity of 'symbol' plus 'retiring place'. There is the setting of the show.

But the usual demand of the setting is that it should shut off a greater or lesser area of the

Fig. 2. A symbol setting for a smithy.

outside world and provide the players with the background of a special world adapted to the best presentation of their show. It is with that department of setting which consists in the making of such a background, in its various degrees of complexity, that I shall concern myself in detail.

We must not here elaborate the above short reference to that far too little explored world of show presentation that comprises the 'Costume' and the 'Symbol' styles of setting. But let me recommend it to your very serious consideration as offering scope for some of the most profound and intimate forms of theatre, and forms dependent upon a tradition of playing far older than any other, though in many details different from that used commonly by actors to-day. Do not let the brevity of this mention deceive you into underrating it.

CHAPTER ONE

Background Setting with no Proscenium

SECTION 1

The 'First Piece of Scenery', an Introduction to Stage-carpentry

We begin by considering the Background Setting without a proscenium. One of the simplest and most popular forms of background stage we find as far back as the first half of the sixteenth century (Fig. 3). It is still very usable to-day and we shall discuss a variant for modern use.

Once the isolating power of a background is learnt, sides tend to grow to it, as Fig. 4, again based on old prints, suggests.

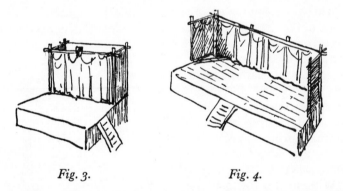

Fig. 3.   *Fig. 4.*

In Fig. 5 these sides turn back and (probably) engage with the walls of a hall.

And then the modification of a central opening may be made (Fig. 6).

There in summary is the scope of our first chapter—Background Setting. It will offer, as we extend it, a field of considerable possibilities and we shall find several fundamental points of construction right away which will remain useful knowledge up to the most advanced stages of the carpentry of full scenery.

There are two views to take of the theatrical setting of

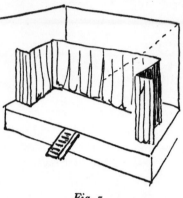

shows. The first is that it should be a complicated thing and make a complete, more or less elaborate surround for the stage, and, with all its details, offer a profusion among which the actor walks. The other is that it should be a small, more or less simple thing, not compact of many details but a single detail in itself, around or before which the action of the scene is hung and

Fig. 5.

which, like the players, takes a part, though a stationary part, in the show.

This qualification 'more or less simple' is important, for in some of the 'less' simple examples, the 'detail' may become a

group or a complex of considerable elaboration (compare for example Fig. 173 and Fig. 184), but such examples scarcely belong to simple setting though the main principles behind them are identical with those we shall discuss here.

Without this distinction between these two points of view upon setting, the term *simple setting* may be incompletely understood.

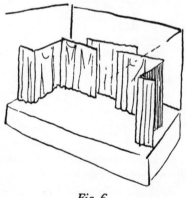

Fig. 6.

Simple setting must not be viewed as a compromise by which a company too poor to afford full scenery makes the best of a bad job. It is a complete subject having its own artistic principles and to be studied for its own intrinsic value as well as for the incidental cheapness its simplicity allows in certain of its forms.

Chief among the principles behind simple setting is the idea of *concentrating* in a small space upon the stage a sufficing commentary upon a given scene to help make a theatrical atmosphere for that scene. This *concentrate* is a vital part of a show. It may be in a sense the central feature, for it is upon it chiefly that the show may rely for a truly valuable theatrical note—a note suggesting what the show really stands for.

It was not for nothing that I mentioned the Maypole in my opening pages. The Maypole is the essence of the Maypole dance. You cannot have a Maypole dance without a Maypole. You cannot have any ritual social ceremony without the ritual objects. The Maypole is the essence of the Maypole dance; our simple detail of setting should be the *essence* of the scene. The setting-designer's job is to reduce the setting to that essence and body it forth in actuality upon his stage.

I would emphasize that it is from that point of view that the whole subject of simple setting is treated in this book. After the preliminary stages, however, we shall find that the essential significance of the detail is not our only concern and that there arises a second consideration—namely the provision of an adequate surround for that detail. Or, if the surround is a fixed condition imposed upon us, the most fitting adaptation of the detail to that surround.

Detail and Surround then are the themes of this book, sometimes one will be played, sometimes the other, sometimes both. But whenever the detail is discussed it is by its essential significance that it stands or falls; becomes a theatrical setting or just a makeshift for a more affluent style.

If then the nature of the detail is so important, the approach which we now make is through a vital part of our subject for it concerns a smallish central screen standing upon an otherwise bare platform. But if the idea above be taken, this screen will be seen to have the potentiality of bearing (according to our use of it) a quintessence of the setting of our scene, a concentration upon a smaller area of all that matters, a poster to advertise our intention, capable of as subtle artistry in its design as anything in the world.

This note as to the value and significance of what we are to discuss is given at length because we are soon to be concerned with many practical details of carpentry, dimension and arrangement. It must not be that, Martha-like, we study these many things as ends in themselves, forgetting that the technique is merely the means of an art. My reader's attitude should be, 'How can I turn these methods to my ends?' But I shall rarely find space here to venture to suggest what those ends should be. My concern is with the methods.

Let us approach the constructional problem with an examination of the most elementary piece of setting, let us take the type of Fig. 3—the simple background screen with a curtain hung upon it—as our 'first piece of scenery'. We have to consider the most practical form for it and a method of building it that shall suit its job.

The dimensions, which are our first consideration, are for

Fig. 7.

settlement in each individual case; in general, however, we may take it that the screen should be above the actors' height; let us say between eight and ten feet. Its length depends, among other things, on its height and on making a well-proportioned rectangle. If we fix ten feet for the height, let us avoid twenty feet for the length, for that makes a rectangle of two squares, and one considered displeasing in proportion. If we avoid fifteen feet (which makes one and a half squares) and settle on ten feet by sixteen feet we have something of fairly satisfactory proportion on which to work—a larger screen perhaps than is needed for some small stages, but one very suitable to introduce us to our problems (Fig. 7).

Settings are generally constructions of a temporary nature, and so the lighter and more portable this screen is the better.

A ten by sixteen feet screen is cumbersome to move, even if only from the workshop to the stage, and if there happens to be a door on the way which is not ten feet high, or an awkward curve in a passage, our piece of scenery must be taken apart before it can be used.

So a ten-foot by sixteen-foot screen must fold.

If it folds in half it becomes a ten-foot by eight-foot surface —which is still too large. It must fold in three. If we cut it into three we have two sections of five feet and one of six feet, and, making the six-foot frame the centre, and hingeing the two five-foots on either side, we have a scheme, details of which we can readily examine.

But before we consider the hingeing, how do we build the three frames, and of what sort and size should the wood be? Let us look first at the construction and then we may go on to see how to use and develop it.

There is a tradition behind the construction of stage scenery, and you can tell at a glance whether even a simple frame is the work of an initiate or not. If you can build scenery that looks like scenery from behind you are likely to have something that is practical, easy to handle, and lasting. If not, your work will be too flimsy or too heavy. Let us initiate ourselves in this tradition.

The nicest product of stage-carpenter's tradition is the design for the 'flat', almost ideal in its simplicity and the rightness of every part for its job. But a true flat is not for the inexperienced carpenter, though it is only a screen of canvas on a wooden frame and is, in some form, the chief element of every scenic construction. Before we inquire into the subtleties of a full flat, let us consider its simpler ancestor, this ordinary frame.

First, the wood with which to build it. In the theatre nearly all framing construction is carried out in a standard cut of timber, and its measure is three inches wide by one inch thick, and so 'three-by-one' comes to be one of the commonest terms of the workshop. This 'three-by-one' is *selected* pine. And it is well worth paying a fraction of a penny more per foot for a better quality—'green' soft-fibred wood makes a very flimsy structure.

25

You will probably buy your wood planed and not rough. In any case the carpenter should take off as few shavings as possible from the face of the wood (the three-inch side) so that the thickness (the one-inch side) should be as great as possible when you come to assemble your parts. So you make for strength and stiffness.

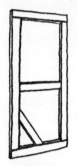

Fig. 8.
*One leaf of
the screen.*

Now for your plan. The two sides and two ends of each frame we may as well begin to call by their right theatrical names. The two long vertical sides are the *stiles* and the two short horizontal ends, the *top* and *bottom rails*.

Across the width of this rectangle we set a horizontal cross-piece to strengthen the stiles; this is almost instinctive and we have a rectangle crossed like an H. But we have to think of the strains and stresses of use, and principal among these is the diagonal strain tending to pull the rectangle into a diamond, so that it is 'out of square', and to counteract this, we plan a cross-corner brace at one of the corners. It is of no great consequence, at the moment, which corner.

Now we are set. Our plan is made (Fig. 8). Our next thought is of the method of jointing the members together.

There is one especial requirement of the corner joints and that is that they should not allow the frame to 'wind'. A

Fig. 9. A 'winder'.

winding frame is one that has twisted so that its top and bottom rails are no longer on the same plane. You can notice this best when the frame is lying flat on the ground (Fig. 9). The evil of this condition is that if you join a flat to either side of a 'winder', it will pull one forward and incline the other back, which in practice becomes so unsightly that the wisest course is always to scrap a winder.

To prevent winding, the 'mortise and tenon' joint (Fig. 10)

26

is far more effective than the 'halve' joint (Fig. 11). Of the two varieties of mortise and tenon joints the 'open' (shown in Fig. 10) is easier to cut than the 'closed', and is sufficiently strong for small frames like these, though for a full-sized flat, a closed joint would be far and away surer and more useful.

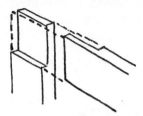

Fig. 10. An open mortise and tenon joint.

Fig. 11. A halved joint.

The next point is, in which member shall be the mortise or cleft, and in which the tenon or tongue. There is great need to place these correctly—and here we enter the subtleties of theatrical technique and formulate a rule useful even in the most advanced construction. The tenons must be cut on the stiles and the mortises in the rails. Let us notice why.

Look at Fig. 12. If we consider the lower edge of the frame in this diagram, we see, on our left corner, the stile is set correctly into the bottom rail, and on the right, the bottom rail is set wrongly into the stile. If now this frame is set upright on the stage, with all its weight on the bottom rail, and subject to the various draggings and skatings on this 'keel', we shall see that the bottom end of the right-hand

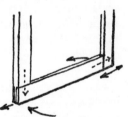

Fig. 12. The correct and incorrect jointing of the bottom rail.

stile is far more likely to suffer splitting out and splintering than that of the left-hand stile, because the weight of the right side of the frame rests on the end grain of the stile, which stands directly on the ground. On the left side, however, the weight is transmitted through the shoulders of the tenon on to the bottom rail whose contact with the ground is parallel, not vertical, to its fibres, and so the rail acts as a sort of sledge-runner to the frame, and indeed, the method of moving a full-sized flat from its place in the pack to its place on the stage is to *run* it, in the language of the theatre, on this sledge or keel-like lower edge. The bottom rail, then, should run straight through from edge to edge of the frame and the stiles be set into it.

Even then, in view of the possibility of the end of the rail running into a nail-head or some such projection on the

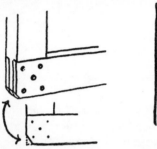

Fig. 13. The chamfering
of the corner.

Fig. 14. A simple closed mortise
and tenon joint.

stage, and ripping a horizontal sliver off the bottom edge, a certain amount of further protection is secured by chamfering an eighth or three-sixteenths of an inch off the corners (as in Fig. 13), so increasing the resemblance to the turned-up ends of a sledge-runner. But before this can be done the parts must be assembled.

Our next step is to incorporate the centre rail between the two stiles, and here clearly the rail must carry the tenons and the stiles be mortised (Fig. 14).

Finally we have to consider the cross-corner brace which holds the frame square. Here the pressure on both ends of the brace is direct and not twisting, and the joint is perfectly adequate if the simpler 'halve' method is used. To do what Fig. 15 shows, the stiles and rails should be assembled, laid flat and tested for squareness, then the corner brace, laid on at an angle of forty-five degrees across the corner from the centre of the rail, should be marked for length and angle of end, while the stile and rail are marked to receive it. Those joints are cut and the whole frame is ready to be glued and screwed.

Concerning glueing, it is very worth while to remember this adage:

> *If the glue's too thick*
> *It will not stick:*
> *If the glue's too cold*
> *It will not hold.*

It is even of assistance to the joint to hold the members over the gas-ring that has heated your glue, for a moment or two,

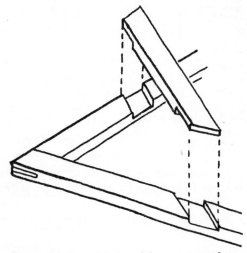

Fig. 15. The halve jointing of the cross-corner brace.

to warm the wood before brushing the hot glue on it. And in brushing glue, remember that as you rub it in with the brush, it begins to foam; watch for that, it is a good augury for its sticking. Work it till it thickens to that little foam every time.

Five screws are placed in a quincunx at each joint, and when the glue has set (that is, in twenty-four hours) your frame can be finished by chamfering the bottom corners with a chisel thrust.

So much for each individual frame. Now for the assembled trio of frames. We plan the corner braces so as to support all four corners of the folded mass, as you see in Fig. 16.

In a single frame, the corner at which the brace is fixed is largely immaterial, but here the braces can be so arranged that, in the folded mass, each of the four corners will be spanned by a brace of one or other of the frames, so ensuring the strength of the pack. See the dotted lines in Fig. 16. We are now ready to face the problem of hingeing the three pieces together.

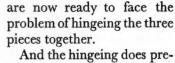

And the hingeing does present a problem. For should you fold Fig. 16 as shown in Fig. 17 something will break when you try to force the last leaf to—you will rip off the hinges and split the wood of the stile.

Similarly, though in a less degree, at the fold of the leaf that comes directly against the centre one, the thickness of *the flap of the hinge itself* presents an obstacle to complete closing. It follows that we must *inset* the flaps of this hinge (Fig. 18).

Fig. 16. The three leaves of the screen, showing the folding and the disposition of the corner braces.

The folding of the third flap is not so simple. There are two

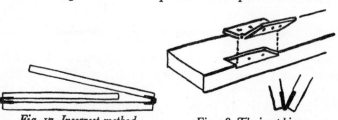

Fig. 17. Incorrect method of hingeing.

Fig. 18. The inset hinge.

ways out of the difficulty, both very useful to store in one's mind for future use.

The first is (Fig. 19) to hinge a compensating strip of wood, an inch square in section, to the edge of the centre frame and to hinge the outermost frame to that strip. Note that this necessitates making the centre frame an inch narrower—5 feet

11 inches instead of 6 feet—if we wish to keep the length of our open screen exactly as before.

Such is the usual method of hingeing together three flats when the outer two are together wider than the centre one.

And it has the advantage that, in travelling, those faces of the flats bearing the canvas are inwards, and so more protected. Moreover the cracks between the flats may be covered with a canvas strip, so that when opened out flat, a plain unbroken surface reaches across the whole three with no sign of a join.

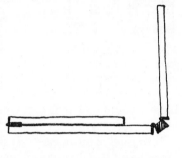

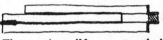

We shall not, however, be especially anxious to conceal the joins between our frames if we propose to use them only to support a loose curtain, and our problem can be equally

Fig. 19. A possible, correct method of folding, using a compensating strip.

well solved by hingeing the third frame so that it folds the reverse way—that is, to the back and not to the front of the centre

Fig. 20. The screen in use, part folded, seen from behind.

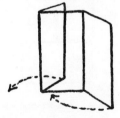

Fig. 21. The only method of folding for travelling if ordinary hinges are used. This forbids the arrangement shown in Fig. 20.

frame. But by this time we are beginning to see something of the stage possibilities of this folding screen, and at the back of

31

our minds there may be already the notion that, on certain occasions at least, we could get a useful variation of setting by standing the screen *partly folded* instead of flat (Fig. 20).

Fig. 22. A once-popular form of note-case involving the principle of the screen hinge.

If we hinge the third leaf with the same type of hinge as the first forward-folding leaf, that possibility will be for ever precluded, for the leaf could only be made to fold one way (Fig. 21). What we need is a hinge that will permit of the leaf being folded either way. If we could find such an ingenious hinge, our problem would be solved, and we should have a very useful unit of stage scenery.

Now, such a hinge exists. It does not seem to be well enough known and it is far too little used on the amateur stage. This is a great pity, for besides being an arrangement of the most delightful ingenuity, it is a valuable accessory to the carpenter's store.

Let us see how it works and how it is fixed—though to grasp its principle at first sight is surprisingly difficult, it acts

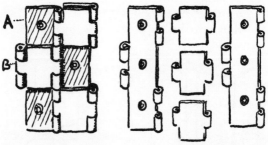

Fig. 23. The screen hinge, assembled, and in its five parts.

in fact as magically as those double-flapped note-cases we used to delight in a few years ago, with two tapes crossed on one flap and two tapes parallel on the other—descendant of a centuries-old Chinese puzzle. The principle of the puzzle applied in metal is no less ingenious. It is called the Screen Hinge.

In Fig. 22, on the right is the note-case, and on the left a special adaptation by which one can follow its transition to the method of the screen hinge. In Fig. 23 is the screen hinge;

32

on the right, in its five pieces and on the left, assembled; the shaded and unshaded parts on the assembled hinge correspond with those upon the left-hand diagram in Fig. 22, and have the same attachments. Upon this assembled hinge there are also two points indicated in its length, *A* and *B*. When it is attached and working, the plan at *A* on a left turn, is as in Fig. 24, with the plan at *B* on the same turn. On the reverse turn, the plans at those two levels are shown in Fig. 25.

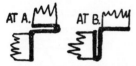

Fig. 24. *Plan of the screen*
hinge on a left turn.

Fig. 25. *Plan of the screen*
hinge on a right turn.

To fix a screen hinge certain points must be observed in a particular order or the inexperienced carpenter may be driven to the verge of insanity.

The proper way is to take the hinge, as shown on the left of Fig. 23. Place the left-hand flap against the edge of one of the frames you wish to hinge together. Insert two screws in the visible holes. Now reverse the hinge, that is, shut it up and then open it out the other way, with the loose flap to the left (your hinge will then appear exactly as in the figure again, but with the screw-heads now concealed and in the right-hand flap). The third or centre screw-hole in the original flap is now exposed. Insert screw. Next place the second of the frames beside the first so that they are either face to face or back to back. Insert two screws through the visible holes in the *other* flap. Open out your screen, swinging one leaf right over until you have folded it up again on the opposite side of the other. Your last screw-hole will then be exposed in the centre of the second flap of the hinge (now on the right-hand side once more), and a screw in this last hole finishes the job.

When we have assembled the three frames and so provided ourselves with a most flexible and useful unit of stage scenery, let us take it on the stage and consider how it can be fixed and held in place.

Our requirement is for a strut or brace, on the same principle as the cross-corner brace, but at right angles to the back of the screen, whose function shall be to preserve the squareness of the angle between the upright screen and the stage. It would be more correct to say 'to preserve a right angle between the upright screen and the horizontal plane', because some stages slope up towards the back—that is to say they are 'raked'—and to stand scenery at right angles to their surface is, in fact, to lean it forward. That has an important bearing on the hingeing of the brace, but for the moment let us turn

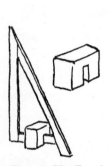

Fig. 26. The French brace with its brace-weight.

Fig. 27. The French brace, in its working position, and folded back.

to the brace itself. In Fig. 26 is a right-angled triangle made in 'three-by-one', with the lower end of the hypotenuse reaching to a point three inches below the bottom of its horizontal rail to provide a foot. Over the rail a metal brace-weight or a sandbag may be hung. This brace is hinged at the back of the screen as in Fig. 27. The foot of the brace and a point in the bottom rail of the screen should be 'halved' (like the joint in Fig. 11) to allow the brace to close flush when it is folded in so as not to hinder the folding of the screen itself.

This particular type of brace, which is called the *French brace*, is not the only one used in the theatre, nor is it the most general, but for this three-fold screen it is the most useful and has the merit of being simple and not demanding for its fixing screws which damage the floor.

If we now provide the inner stile of each outer leaf with French braces, we can set up our screen securely on the stage even when it is opened out flat (Fig. 28).

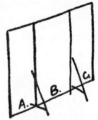

If we propose to set our screen part-folded, we must take care to screw the brace-hinges as in Fig. 29 (these hinges do not require to be inset) so that we shall be able to open them past the right angle, and slope them back out of sight (Fig. 30).

We are not likely to bring such a simple piece of scenery on to a raked stage; we are designing for the horizontal hall-platform; but to adapt it to the raked stage there would have to be a modification in the hingeing of the brace.

Fig. 28. The complete screen braced flat, seen from the back.

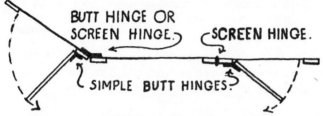

Fig. 29. The proper position and character of each hinge.

If the stage is raked, the French-braced screen will lean forward. This angle must be corrected and the way is simple.

It should not be done by the wasteful expedient of cutting the foot of the brace short, so making it unsuitable for use on a flat stage again, but by 'kicking the hinge' —that is to say, fixing the brace to the lower hinge a little out of its proper alignment so that when opened it 'kicks' its toe up a little. Fig. 33 illustrates diagrammatically what happens. In Fig. 31 is shown the frame with the normal brace folded in and the hinges in their usual position. In Fig. 32 the whole brace is slightly canted sideways before the flap of the lower hinge is screwed to it. The brace now opens as shown in the side view

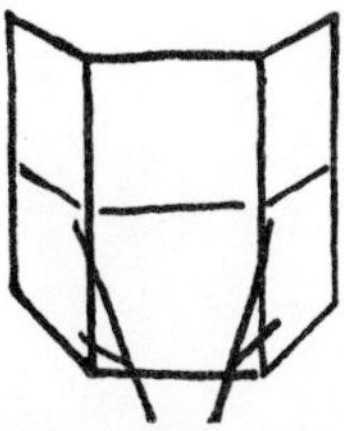

Fig. 30. The complete screen braced part-folded, seen from the back.

35

in Fig. 33, raising its foot slightly; it follows that the screen will stand more or less upright according to the amount that the hinge is 'kicked'.

If you thoughtlessly saw off the end of your brace-foot to accommodate it to a raked stage, you will of course never be

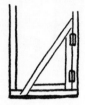  

Fig. 31. 'Kicking the hinge' (a). A normally placed French brace.

Fig. 32. 'Kicking the hinge' (b). The brace tilted and the lower hinge screwed nearer to the edge of the brace.

Fig. 33. 'Kicking the hinge' (c). The whole piece set on a raked stage and viewed from the side.

able to set your screen upright again when you return to the level platform. You can accommodate any rake by 'kicking' the hinge correspondingly, and when you replace the hinge,

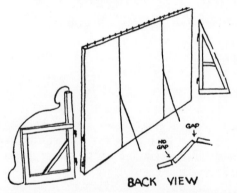

Fig. 34. Two forms of side extension to the screen, and curtain-nails at the top.

suit the screen once more to the level with no waste. Frequent alteration of the hinge damages the wood by pitting it with screw-holes so that the old holes must be plugged up with scraps of wood before new holes can be truly driven.

36

So much for the simple three-fold screen without trimmings. It is, however, already capable of one or two quite amusing elaborations in ingenious hands.

Consider Fig. 34. We are viewing our screen in diagrammatic form from behind. Along its top edge a row of nails is now to be noticed, upon which the rings of a curtain may be hooked to drape the screen.

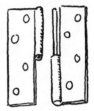

Fig. 35. A loose-butt hinge.

But the chief extension of its decorative possibilities is in the addition of the small 'flipper' by which the straight vertical ends may be swept down more softly in a decorative curve or in a swift unbroken slope from top to stage. The flippers are shaped frames covered with canvas. One triangular version (shown at the far end of the screen) is much like a French brace in construction. An alternative, a scrolled shape (shown at the nearest end of the screen) is more elaborate and is provided with a 'profile' of plywood in which the shape is cut. That is to say, before the square frame is canvassed, a strip of ply is nailed along the side and the top (and if the strip is wide it may be supported by an extension from the wood of the frame). The whole is canvassed and painted and, lastly, the ply is cut to the intended shape with a fretsaw or a padsaw.

These flippers are generally temporary additions to a screen, and are removed for travelling. They may, however, be required to be hinged on in order that they may stand at an angle to the screen itself when in use. Is there a hinge that will fulfil these two requirements? Fig. 35 shows a 'loose butt' hinge whose pin is fixed securely to one flap, while the other flap is separate and its slot drops over the pin of the first flap like an eye on a hook. Provided with such hinges, the flipper may be removed at will or, when fixed, it can be set at any angle within a quarter of a circle—that is, moved forward from a position in which it is parallel to the main screen to a position where it is turned nearly at right angles to it (if it turned farther it would show its back). But what

Fig. 36. A reversible pin hinge.

if, on occasion, we need to fold the flipper backwards? We shall then use, instead of the 'loose butt' hinge, the 'reversible pin' hinge shown in Fig. 36, whose flap may be made to fold either way by alteration of the pin from side to side. When the screen is to be packed away, the pin can be withdrawn and the flipper detached.

Notice that, if the screen should be canvassed and a flipper is turned forward (as in the little plan in Fig. 34) there will be no gap occasioned between flipper and screen, but if it is

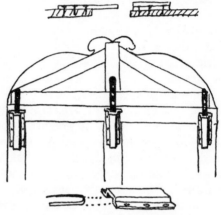

Fig. 37. A top extension for the screen.

turned back there will be a gap which may interfere with a possible painted design on the piece.

Before leaving the 'loose butt', warning should be given to avoid knocking the pin out of alignment, or the fixing of the flipper becomes a matter of trouble and wasted time. Further, it is useful to use hinges of different sizes in the upper and lower positions on such a flipper. If one pair of hinges is large and the other small, one has only, when engaging the flaps, to insert one pin at a time, the longer first; this is better than having them the same size, and trying to engage them simultaneously—a trick none too easy if you have a flipper of any size.

Finally let us consider an occasion, as in Fig. 37, when it is decided to provide a top extension to the centre leaf of the screen. In such a case, having removed the curtain nails at the top edge, you employ a piece built on the same principle as a flipper and provided with metal prongs at the back which engage in sockets screwed on the back of the centre leaf of the screen. In a wide frame it is occasionally helpful to add a central stile to take a centre socket, as in the figure.

Fig. 38. A plain screen, curtained.

Fig. 39. A plain screen, canvassed.

Fig. 40. The screen part-folded and curtained.

These metal extension fittings can be bought for a shilling, plug and socket together. Failing such a thing at hand, in an emergency a quite satisfactory substitute is an eighteen-inch length of 'three-by-one' screwed securely across the join where each plug and socket would have been.

Fig. 41. The screen, canvassed, part-folded and with extensions.

Fig. 42. The plain screen, canvassed, and painted for a room setting.

We have now an element of setting upon which several variations can be played. In Fig. 38 is the simple screen, set flat and hung with a curtain; in Fig. 39 is the same screen canvassed and painted with a formal pattern—notice the two decorative finials at the top corners, nailed on in ply. In Fig. 40 is the curtained screen set with the leaves slightly infolded, and (Fig. 41) the painted canvas screen, in-folded and provided with a profiled top extension and returning flippers. In Fig. 42 is the plain canvassed screen painted with a

39

suitable door and window, to stand for the scenery of a full chamber-set—a convention admirable in its economy and well worth trying. In Fig. 43 is another arrangement, draped. And lastly the simple three-fold screen is arranged and draped to supply an asymmetrical setting, finished with a profile flower-vase and a ball-finial (Fig. 44).

Fig. 43. *The part-folded screen with extensions, curtained.*

Fig. 44. *The part-folded screen, draped and with additional details.*

So much then for our first unit of theatrical scenery. Simple as it appeared to be at first, we have come upon nearly a score of technical details of primary practical importance, and even then we have given no more than an allusion to the finer details of canvassing and profiling. Moreover, we have suggested a new field for style in setting, or at least a field very little explored to-day, and we are still only on the fringes of this division of setting that I have called Background Setting. Let us next go on to more elaborate examples of the type, where sides as well as a larger back come to be used, and discuss the subject of *hanging* background curtains, and the arrangement and fixing of their lines.

SECTION 2

The Simple Side-hung Curtain

We are still dealing with a plain hall whose only contribution to our show is a bare platform across the end.

We have discussed the Background pure and simple. Next comes its development and the growth of sides.

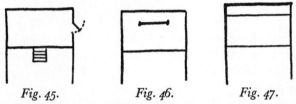

Fig. 45.   *Fig. 46.*   *Fig. 47.*

The players have entered up to now by steps from the front or by a door on the stage (Fig. 45).

The development of scenery is towards the isolation of the acting-area. A movement not without its disadvantages, and one which leads, in the end, to a reaction in the attempt to

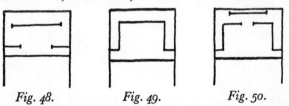

Fig. 48.   *Fig. 49.*   *Fig. 50.*

re-establish the contact between the players and the audience. At present, however, we must follow the trend and discuss the increasingly exclusive 'nest' for the players, from which the extraneous world is more and more pushed out.

To the empty platform (Fig. 45) we added the small background screen (Fig. 46). We proceed to consider a fuller background (Fig. 47), a development thereof (Fig. 48), then

41

background plus sides (Fig. 49) and then the modification in Fig. 50, and what it implies.

For this we shall have to devise a much simpler way of support for curtains than standing screens—and that is 'side-hanging'.

Fig. 51. Forms of support
(a) Self-standing.

Fig. 52. Forms of support
(b) Standing-braced.

To understand the term 'side-hanging' look at Figs. 51 to 54, where the four methods of supporting pieces of scenery on the stage are shown. In Fig. 51 is the simplest method, where a hinged piece is 'self-standing'; in Fig. 52 is the method with which we are familiar from our screen, 'standing-braced'; in

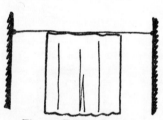

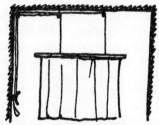

Fig. 53. Forms of support
(c) Side-hung.

Fig. 54. Forms of support
(d) Top-hung.

Fig. 53 is a 'side-hung' curtain; in Fig. 54 is the 'top-hanging' method which entails the use of a border to hide the lines and gear.

Let us now suppose that a show is to be put on in a hall similar to that with which we began, save that the existing background to the platform is so inconsistent with our show that we wish to cover it from one side of the stage to the other. We can avoid going the length of making and carting sufficient frames to hang our curtains on if permission can be obtained to make two fixtures, one in either side wall, between which we can string a line wherefrom to hang our curtains.

Because the rest is so simple it occasionally comes about that this one difficulty is not properly thought about. It is imperative that the anchor points of the line should be sufficiently strong.

Let us consider the nature of this curtain line and then the method of anchoring it.

First, the line itself must not be capable of stretching. It must be able to stand considerable strain without breaking, and so a wire cable and not a hemp rope is needed.

Secondly, this cable must be strung so tightly that even with the weight of the curtains upon it, it will not sag to any

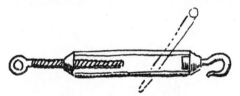

Fig. 55. A wire-strainer.

great extent. And so we incorporate a wire-strainer at one or both ends.

A wire-strainer (Fig. 55) consists of an open body, at one end of which is a swivel-hook, and at the other an eye on a long screw shank, which can be screwed farther and farther into the body, by turning that body over and over; if necessary, with the help of a lever thrust through the body.

A wire cable is often an unfamiliar thing to an amateur stage-hand, and, given the wire and the strainer, the question is how to fix the one strongly and neatly to the end of the other. A rope can be spliced or knotted, but a wire cable is a most ungrateful object to tie a knot in, and splicing wire is a job of work. How then can it be fixed?

One property of all stranded cables is that if the end is doubled back on itself and lightly gripped, the strands on the one part will interlock with those of the standing part and the loop will not slip until the gripping agent itself breaks. For this gripping agent you may wind wire round your union, or a strong thin line (Fig. 56), but special wire-rope grips are made for this purpose (for fourpence each) by which you can

Fig. 56. A loop held by gripping the inter-locking strands of the two parts of the cable.

Fig. 57. A wire-rope grip.

make a fixture as strong as the tensile power of the rope itself (Fig. 57).

To make a really good job the ends of the cable itself should first be 'whipped' to prevent the strands fraying out. The ends of all working ropes on the stage, wire or other, should be so treated, especially if they are to be led through pulleys,

Fig. 58. Whipping an end (1).

when a knotted end would prevent their passage. The details of 'whipping the end' are shown in Figs. 58 to 63.

With about two feet of whipping twine in the left hand and the rope to be served in the right, overlap the ends of the two for a distance of three or four inches. Secure the twine near the end of the rope between the thumb and finger of the right hand (Fig. 58). With the left hand begin to wind the rest of the twine round the rope-end in the direction shown by the arrow, till you have reached the point suggested in Fig. 59, that is between half a dozen and a dozen turns.

Holding the turns with the left hand, take the free end of the whipping twine in the right and lay it along the rope securing it with the right thumb then continue the winding as before (Fig. 60), but now trapping the fresh end of the twine with each turn.

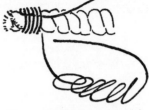

Fig. 59. Whipping an end (2).

Fig. 61 shows this winding, with two turns taken over the new end of the twine. Continue winding for a similar number of turns as before and you reach the position shown in Fig. 62. There remains only to pull the last-folded-back end of the twine in the direction of the arrow so that your job appears as in Fig. 63 and to trim off the ends.

Fig. 60. Whipping an end (3).

To keep the eye of a loop open a 'thimble' may be used, Fig. 64. The thimble is gently opened to take the end of the wire-strainer and pinched to again. If the thimble has no join, a shackle (Fig. 65) is used to link thimble and ring. The whipped cable is led round the thimble with six inches of end to spare. A grip is screwed over the two wires close to the thimble, and a second grip four or five inches along (Fig. 66). The other end of the

Fig. 61. Whipping an end (4).

cable may be similarly supplied with a thimble, either for a
second strainer if the span is long, or for a hook to fasten
directly to the wall-ring. Thus you have a length of wire

Fig. 62. Whipping an end (5).   Fig. 63. Whipping an end (6).

cable ending in a wire-strainer hook at one end and a plain
hook at the other, and long enough to fit just comfortably
into two rings fixed in the side walls, when the strainer is
out to its fullest extent.

The next point, and a very important one, is the firm an-

Fig. 64. A Thimble.   Fig. 65. A Shackle.

choring of these rings to the walls. The rings must be fixtures.
If you happen to be lucky enough to find a column or stan-
chion of sufficient strength, in the right position, you may of
course encircle it with a couple of loops of wire and thread the
ring through these. You should take care to pack your wire

Fig. 66. Method of attaching wire rope.

loops with pieces of wood to prevent the wire cutting into the
column.

If you have, however, a bare wall-face in which to fix your
eye, you have two alternatives; to use a specially prepared
eye-bolt cemented into the wall or to put a threaded eye-bolt

completely through the wall and fix a plate and a nut on the other end.

Your curtains will most probably be hung in folds. Their material we will discuss when we talk about the full curtain set, but the method of fixing is somewhat different here from that of the full set.

From the strained wire the curtains may be hung by rings or hooks sewn behind the top of the curtain. If the rings are

Fig. 67. Wrong method of attaching curtain rings.

sewn directly to the top of the curtain, they and the wire will show and the curtain will hang in curves at the top, and its folds will not be equal except after some arrangement (Fig. 67). But if the curtain be gathered first and sewn on to a webbing band, placed an inch or two from the upper edge of the curtain, its folds can be regularized as they are sewn on, and, if the rings are sewn about the middle of the webbing, its top will hide the wire (Figs. 68 and 69).

The lower hem of the curtain may be made deep enough to have a chain threaded through it as a weight to help the

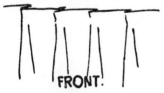 

Fig. 68. Correct method of attach-
ing curtain rings.

Fig. 69. Correct method of attach-
ing curtain rings, back view.

graceful hang of the curtain. Bright chain for weighting curtains can be bought at between 2s. 9d. and 1s. 5d. per dozen yards according to size.

Of course a curtain with rings must be threaded on the wire before the latter is hooked across; a curtain with hooks (either plain hooks or snap hooks, for which see Fig. 74) can be hung from an already-strained wire.

47

If the curtains are heavy and the span of the cable fairly long, noticeable sag in the middle may be unavoidable. Then a brace, or a couple of braces, on the system of clothes-line props will be needed.

Any experience you may have had with clothes-lines and props will have taught you the ugly trick the upper end of the prop has of slipping sideways along the line, if it is not directly vertical, and so, on the curtain cable, to hold the upper end of the brace in place, a couple of rope-grips are necessary, with room for the brace head to fit between them.

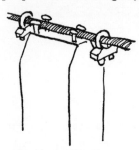

Fig. 70. Detail of the head of a line-prop.

The brace itself should be of $2'' \times 2''$ or $3'' \times 2''$ batten, and either notched like the clothes prop at its upper end, or tapered and provided with four screws between which the cable may pass (Fig. 70). If the lower end is in danger of slipping, it must be screwed to the stage, or provided with a brace-foot (see index) and weighted.

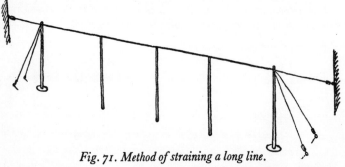

Fig. 71. Method of straining a long line.

Circumstances may demand this simple form of background curtain, but in a considerably longer stretch than anything we have yet considered. Either in a large hall or in the open air, it may need to be forty or fifty feet long. Then the direct strain on the two anchor points will be too great and the principle of guy-ropes on a horizontal bar should be adopted (Fig. 71). Then the pull at the tent-peg-like anchor

48

points on the ground is at right angles. The wall-anchors are merely strained sufficiently to carry an extension curtain from the end post to the wall.

Finally, as one example of the many ways in which the principles noted above may be developed in practice, it is worth while considering the arrangement in Fig. 72, where a

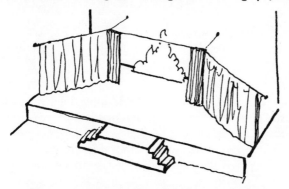

Fig. 72. A useful simple set needing four wall-rings.

strained wire across the stage is pulled out of the straight, or brailed back, at two points by a couple of subsidiary wires, anchored to points in the back wall. The curtains on the diagonal sides, or 'wings', are permanent but that on the centre wire may part in the middle, and disclose a set scene if and when required. Of which more later. As it is, this form suggests 'sides' as well as 'back', and supplies a suitable transition step to our next development.

SECTION 3

The Side-hung 'Arras' Setting—The Guy-rope Set— The Birth of the Proscenium Arch—An Introduction to Sight-lines

Now let us return to the simple side-hung background on a platform. If we extend our problem to the masking of the sides as well as the back as we predicted in Figs. 4 and 5, we may, in solving it, take two or three steps forward; for, once we have accepted the need for sides, the fittings necessary for their hanging will take us straight to a new factor, the proscenium arch.

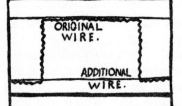

Fig. 73. Ground plan of an 'arras' set.

It is obvious that if we have three sides of our acting-area curtained, the presentation to some of the audience of the front edge of the side curtains is unpleasant, and it is not satisfactory to see the actors walking down the wings, around the down-stage edge of the side curtain each time they have to enter the acting-area. Further, the 'wings', as we come to call these off-stage spaces beside the acting-area, are difficult to light in the same key as the stage, and they provide a distraction. So we make two innovations; we bring on the actors through the curtain wall and we *return* the sides to *mask* the wings.

What beyond our simple back-curtain cable do we need for this? Simply a parallel cable at the front of the stage and a pair of battens to ride between the two wires.

We have reached at this point a landmark in our story, well-known under the name of the 'arras set'. The 'side-hung

50

arras set', about which we are speaking, is the simplest form. Its disadvantages in practice are its inflexibility and a tendency to sag if any but light hangings are used.

These are its details: at the down-stage or front limit of the set is stretched a second and parallel wire in exactly the same way as the first (Fig. 73). At the side limits of the set, for

Fig. 74. A spring
hook.

Fig. 75. Detail of end of
side batten.

side curtains, a batten of $3'' \times 1''$ is hung by means of a snap- or spring-hook screwed into either end of the batten, or bolted through its width (Figs. 74 and 75), in such a way that the batten hangs edge downwards. To the inner side of either batten, cup-hooks are screwed at

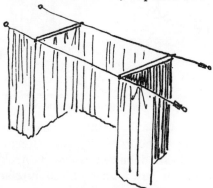

Fig. 76. The side-hung arras set.

intervals to take the rings on the curtain or alternatively, screw-eyes if the web is provided with curtain-hooks.

Then, upon the ends of the down-stage wire may be hung strips of curtain—those returns we mentioned above—whose function is to connect the sides of the set with the sides of the house and mask the passage at the side of the set from the audience (Fig. 76).

51

We have now stepped beyond the mere background into something a little wider, something we might call a 'surround', whose advancing side-arms limit the 'acting-area' much more sharply than before.

But a company may find itself in a position in which, although they desire to use the effect of a surround, they are forbidden or unable to make any fixtures in the side walls of the hall. And so we turn next to the 'Guy-rope' Curtain Set.

It is possible to arrange a useful set very similar to the side-hung curtain set in Fig. 76, with back, sides and front

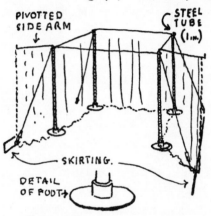

Fig. 77. The 'guy-rope' curtain set.

returns of curtain with a little extra trouble in collecting preliminary gear but without making any attachments to the walls of the stage beyond four screw-eyes in the skirting board below. The arrangement, a form of 'standing-braced' set, is shown in Figs. 77 and 78.

In Fig. 78 is shown a wire cable arranged in a square, with cable-grips pinching the corners into loops. Into each of the four loops is hooked a guy-wire, with a wire-strainer and hook at the farther end. Those four loops at the corners of the square are slipped over the top of four posts, made of metal tube—possibly one inch gas barrel—and are prevented from slipping down the post by a pin inserted through the tube, near the top, as shown in the centre of the square.

The posts are screwed at the lower end into flanges which form feet (Fig. 77, below) and the whole is assembled as in Fig. 77, the guy-ropes being hooked into screw-eyes placed in the skirting-board or the stage, and then tightened by means of the wire-strainers.

Into a socket or strap at the top of each front post is dropped the turned-down end of a metal rod which acts as a pivoted side-arm for the curtains of the returns.

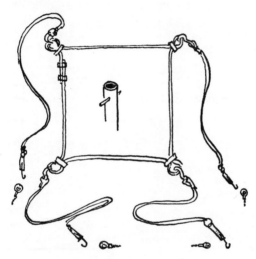

Fig. 78. Details of the guy-rope set.

As I have said, the limitation of such sets is their comparative inflexibility. But there are certain variations to be played upon the theme.

The most important we have already indicated. It was the provision of a central entrance at the back, to make which the curtain is in two equal parts, each drawn off to the side, leaving a central gap, Fig. 79.

Here we come upon something of so special a nature that I think it worth while to turn aside and discuss it. It brings us into the realm of 'Theatre' at once. We have reached the place where we see the possibility of representational changeable scenery to be set in that little inner space at the back.

53

There is reason to believe that at all periods in history when this discovery of scenery was made by various theatrical ages, each building its fate in its own way from simple beginnings, it was made in some manner broadly resembling this. The discovery is of the possibilities that a central back opening, which can be closed at will, has for occasional tableaux which can be hidden by closing the opening and changed before the curtain is withdrawn. It is difficult at first to recognize here the ancestor of our proscenium arch because it is situated at the *back* and not at the front of the stage. But this unfamiliar position for the proscenium, that we think of

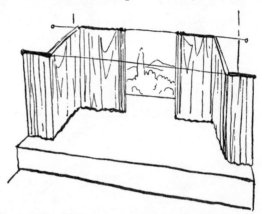

Fig. 79. The side-hung arras set with a centre back opening.

to-day as inseparable from the down-stage part of the acting-area where the footlights are, is quite in order historically. Anciently, the proscenium wall was at the back of the stage, and the scenery was a tiny picture inside it or against it, while the whole extent of the stage walls in front was non-committally decorated, possibly never changed, and suiting every play. These walls embraced the acting-area where the players moved and they were never hidden by a curtain. Without our knowing it, the set we have outlined here is in principle completely traditional and has the counterpart of every one of its details in the first theatrical stages of the Renaissance and again in the theatre of the classical Greeks. The only difference is of material, for, where the walls around the old acting-

area were elaborately built in stone, and decorated with pillars and niches and statues, ours are temporary and of curtain, but in no sense are ours more, or less, non-committal and
general than their solid prototypes. Their distribution and
use are exactly the same.

If we were to seek further and look not at the elaborately-
built stone feats of architecture that were the early theatres,
but at some of the strolling players' settings, or the boy-students' backgrounds of the Middle Ages, we should find evidence of an identical principle.

The Elizabethan theatre, though generally without
scenery upon the main stage, was provided with an 'inner
stage' at the back where tableaux were exposed such as Fer-
dinand playing chess with Miranda in *The Tempest*. And we
have, at least, no evidence to prove that some sort of decking
of this inner stage was not attempted, and a form of scenery
used within its small area. Rather, a knowledge of the working of the theatrical mind leads us to suppose that, given the
opportunity of such a space behind a curtain, it would be
strange indeed if some use were not made of it.

Finally, to return to the Greek theatre, where this form
was first exploited to our present knowledge, we find in con-
temporary accounts, a machine called the *ekkuklema* at
whose exact nature it is only possible to guess, but which
most authorities agree was probably a sort of low platform on
wheels—a truck—upon which a tableau was set behind the
scenes to be drawn on the stage for the inspection of the
audience. Our acquaintance with the Greek stage makes it
difficult to find any access to the acting-area big enough to
admit the passage of such a machine other than the great
central door of the *skene* itself—the central door that later became our 'proscenium arch'. This *skene* was the tiring-house,
built at the back of the stage, and its front wall, with the great
central door was called the 'front of the *skene*' or, in Greek
(*pro*=before) *proskenion*, and later, in Latin, the *proscenium*.

Whence, clearly, our arch of to-day.

So we find ourselves, in spite of the humble beginning, in
step at every move with the old tradition of the theatre, and
although we might have supposed such a setting as I began

to describe to be a mere substitute for the proscenium-framed picture, and to be used only by very impecunious amateur companies, we now perceive that the method has a very dignified ancestry and, in intelligent hands, is one of vital importance to the resources of a modern producer.

Now we are approaching that kind of set which hides extraneous details, and this central opening must be provided with a *backing*. Let us suppose at first a simple curtain backing, not (as shown) a painted ground-row. For this (unless we

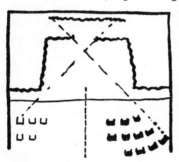

wish to fix the anchorings for a third wire across the back of the stage), nothing more suitable can be found than our simple screen of the last section, standing in any one of its variant forms (as in Fig. 38), but with one especial point observed, however it be set, that the backing must now 'mask'. It must be seen adequately to back the opening from any seat in the

Fig. 80. Plan of stage and front seats showing sight-lines.

house, *especially those side front stalls* which we shall come to find are the most important factors for conditioning the dimensions of stage scenery in the whole theatre. And for that reason, and because we shall need to say so much of them in advanced work, let us consider Fig. 80 so that you may have their point of view on the masking.

Fig. 80 represents a plan of the curtains of this type of set: at the back you see the central opening of a certain width and, beyond it, the backing.

Note that the backing needed to mask this given width of opening is considerably wider than the opening itself, and furthermore, it is even wider than the extra width that the narrowing effect of perspective upon more distant objects would lead us to expect. For the spectator's view-point will vary according to the width of the auditorium, and we have to see that our backing masks adequately when viewed from either of the two most extremely lateral seats. *A backing, then, may need to be three times the width of the opening it masks.*

To your left of the plan are indications of some of those side seats in outline, and a dotted line from the end seat of the front row through the opposite side of the centre opening shows to what point the backing for that opening must reach.

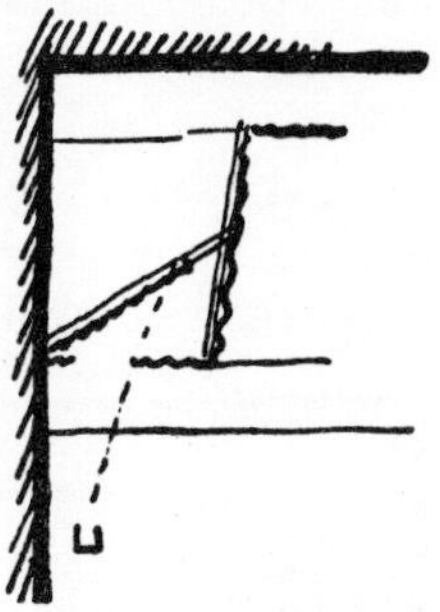

Upon the right of the plan another arrangement of seats is indicated in heavier black. Here it is to be noticed that the sidemost seat is *not* that at the end of the first row, but of the third row, and the sight-line must be taken from there.

Fig. 81. The diagonal backing of an opening in the front return.

A full study of sight-lines is a work of some complexity and must be deferred to another place. We occupy ourselves here with them only for as much longer as is necessary to describe the next development we make in this simple side-hung set. That development is the provision of side-entrances in the curtains.

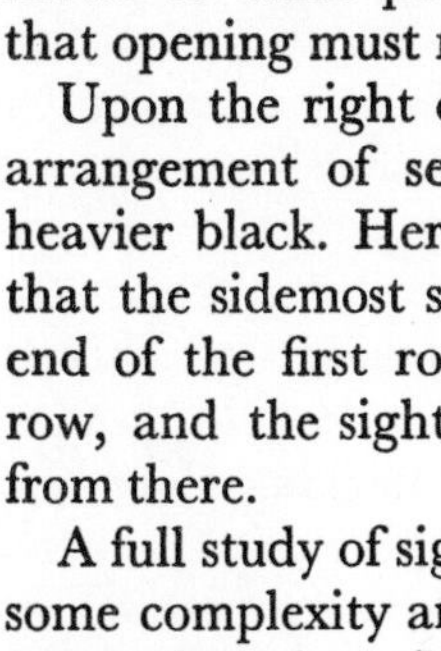

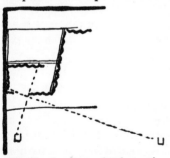

Fig. 82. A common, but less satisfactory, alternative to Fig. 81.

Fig. 81 is a plan of half the stage showing an opening in the side return. For the backing of this opening, a light batten is laid between the anchor-point of the front wire and the batten which carries the side-curtain, and upon this the backing-curtain is hung.

This backing is hung diagonally. Were it hung parallel with the return it would mask just as well from the near corner seat, *but not from the opposite side corner seat.* In Fig. 82 you see the sight-line from this seat and it is clear therefrom that a further curtain would have to be hung on the side wall itself to join the off-stage edge of the parallel backing with the corresponding edge of the return curtain.

Openings in the side curtains of the set are often still more difficult to mask because it will be clear that no backing can be allowed to stretch right across the wing-space, or there would be no room for the actor to get round it as he goes to or from his entrance.

The opening in the side-curtain in Fig. 83 shows a simple parallel backing (with an alternative). Suppose now that the circumstances were such that the wing space was much narrower than in the figure, and the side wall of the house only a little beyond the side-curtain of the set: then there would be either no space to hang the width of backing necessary to mask or there would be just enough for backing alone and nothing to spare for the actor coming to his entrance. If he were allowed to pull the backing curtain aside he would immediately disclose the beyond, and a further backing would be needed to mask the opening caused by this displacement. In such circumstances it is necessary to return the outer end of the backing down-stage at right angles, as you see alternatively marked on the diagram, but generally the most economic arrangement is the diagonal backing to an entrance in the front return as shown in Fig. 81.

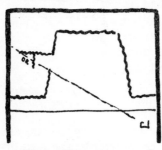

Fig. 83. Alternative ways of backing an opening in the side curtains.

Further developments than these we should generally not attempt with the arras set, or we begin to look as if we were trying to ape a theatre-stage set and failing. Any more enrichment must be in the curtains, their quality and hanging, and in the design of the painted detail that might on occasion be set in the centre-back opening. And it must be an inviolable rule to keep the type of setting pure. Remember its traditional use.

One of the chief limitations of this particular version is that, as no drop-curtain or front 'tabs' can be used on the arras stage, re-arrangement during a show may be difficult. Front tabs should not be used unless they can reach from the stage to the ceiling of the hall, or unless the space between their top and the ceiling is in some way draped or filled in. Without such a top valance it is difficult to hide, or render pleasant to look at, the necessary railway and lines. And to run front cur-tains on the down-stage strained cable of your set is bad psy-chologically. You occupy the attention of your audience with vain speculations about what is going on behind the wall over which they cannot see. Above the curtain-top the upward spill of the stage lights gives away your atmosphere and con-centration, and anyhow the closing of front curtains with so small a 'visible means of support' as your strained wire is sug-gestive of the flimsy and the ill-finished. Moreover, the endless lines, by which that curtain will be worked, will hang in sight and sag, and they will gather up and kick as the linesmen gets ready to close the curtains on a scene—which is a moment of climax and one when it is rank bad presentation to anticipate, or do anything to distract your audience's attention.

If you must have a curtain then your growing idea must rise to the proscenium arch, with its upper part convenient to hide your curtain lines and all upper-workings. Or you must evolve for yourself a new type of front curtain which will not be inconsistent with your standing arras set (one possibility is suggested on p. 71), whose nature and appearance *suggest* a set stood upon a stage, not hung from the ceiling above it. That standing-upon-the-stage appearance is the keynote of the arras set.

We have to confess that, simple as the side-hung curtain method is, there is another version of the arras set that is a great deal more capable of variation in general use, though considerably more elaborate to make. That other version is the 'Standing Arras' proper, for which we must return to a modification of our original frame.

Before that, however, I want to make an interpolation. We have already had to use one or two technical phrases relating to stage positions and directions, it is important that we should pause and define exactly how movement and placing on stage surfaces are indicated in words, so that we may suffer no misunderstanding.

SECTION 4

An Explanation of Stage Directions

In speaking of stage positions I have used certain terms which are mostly self-evident, but in one or two cases are extremely confusing if not understood. They are indispensable in proper use.

Figs. 84, 85 and 86 show these terms.

Fig. 84 shows the plan of a stage and, first of all, emphasizes that the *stage left* is on the *actor's* left as he faces the audience, not on the spectator's left. (This is because the actor is

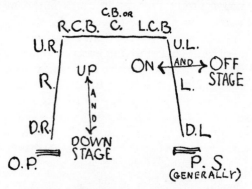

Fig. 84. The subdivisions of the sides of a stage, etc.

presumably facing the auditorium when he reads his script at rehearsals and begins to map his movements, and the directions are addressed to him.)

In order (ostensibly) to avoid confusion, another method is used of designating the sides of the stage, and this is to speak of the *Prompt Side* and the *Opposite Prompt*. The word 'side' in the second expression is almost always dropped and the whole may be further shortened and pronounced 'O.P.' An object situated 'on the O.P.' is *usually* one on the stage right, for the Prompt Corner is generally down near the proscenium on the stage left. But in some theatres, the building makes this inexpedient and the Prompt Side is on the right. A company should always ascertain which is the prompt side of any theatre they use. If the term Prompt Side is used without reference to a special theatre it is to be taken as meaning the *stage left*.

Movements on a stage in a to-and-from direction with regard to the audience, that is, away from or nearer to the footlights, are always described in terms of *height*. This may confuse those who have never met a raked (or sloping) stage, and do not realize that the back of such stages is *higher* than the front. (The rake incidentally is of no practical use whatever now, and should be avoided in building new stages, but in the past it set for us these particular stage directions.) To go 'up-stage', then, is to retire to the *back* of the stage, and to 'come down' is clearly to

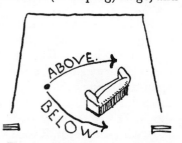

Fig. 85. The correct description of movement.

move to the front. So much is easily understood. But the expression is developed further—a producer will say to an actor, 'Go a little up,' or 'Come down a bit.' These remarks, in the light of this explanation, will be perfectly clear, but, disconnected and in actual life, they may need a little learning before one responds to them automatically. It is essential they should be learnt and used because there are certain circumstances where this form of expression is the only one which unequivocally conveys a meaning, as the following shows:

Imagine an actor and a settee upon a stage. You wish the actor to cross the stage so that he passes the settee on the opposite side to yourself seated in the auditorium. Can you tell him, 'Cross *behind* the settee?' Yes, maybe, *if the settee is facing the audience*, but if it is as in Fig. 85, and the actor's position as represented by the black dot to the stage right of it (and on the same *level*), what then? Clearly to tell the actor to go *be-hind* the settee is equivocal. If he goes round the far side of it, from your point of view, he is passing the *front* of the settee and so cannot clearly be said to go *behind*.

The whole confusion will be laid for ever if the right terms are used and the actor is told to pass *below* the settee—yes, that is the phrase—that is to say, on the *downstage* side of it. (Or alternatively *above* the settee, when he can only pass on the up-stage side, or that more distant from the audience.) This remains equally precise with the settee facing in any direction.

So then (returning to Fig. 84), movements from or to the footlights are said to take place in directions *up* or *down* stage.

Similarly, the lateral movements are described in terms of *on* or *off* stage. *Onstage* is obviously on the stage and in sight—*offstage* is obviously off the stage and hidden in the wings.

These expressions are also used for narrower movements upon the acting-area itself. For instance, an actor standing on the point of the arrow indicating the word 'on' in Fig. 84 should be requested to step towards the centre line of the stage with the words, 'Come *on* a bit'—and to retire in the opposite direction with, 'Go *off* a little.' To ask him to come nearer centre, or go farther from centre is not the same thing for in those cases he would make a diagonal movement towards or from a *point* dead in centre of the stage. But to move 'on' or 'off' signifies movement in the same plane as he occupies at first and either to or from the centre *line* of the stage. A producer is often, and rightly, incensed when an actor whom he tells to *move on a little* comes out of his plane and moves nearer the footlights as well as moving towards the centre line. 'No,' shouts the producer, 'I said *on* not *down*.' And the uninitiated doesn't 'get much change out of that'.

Further, any piece of scenery which is set at right angles to the footlights is said to be set 'directly up-and-down stage', while, in altering a diagonal wing to a position more nearly parallel to the footlights, the stage manager may ask for it to be set 'more on-and-off'.

With the above introduction the initials on Fig. 84 should

be all understandable. 'C' is Centre, and 'R.C.B.' is Right Centre Back.

In Fig. 86 is a plan of the areas of a stage, of great use to have in mind at rehearsals The Centre, Right and Left divisions are obvious, as are the Down- and Up-Centre, etc. Further subdivisions are noted, in smaller letters, which very

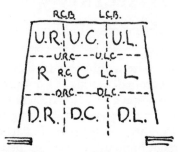

Fig. 86. The names of the areas of a stage.

roughly come upon the junction of the boundaries of the main divisions, these subdivisions are Up Right-Centre, Down Right-Centre, etc.

On a large stage and with a large cast in a crowd scene, it is often helpful to square up the stage as in Fig. 86 with chalk, and then subdivide each square into quarters numbered from one to four, and to give each player a large, plainly numbered label. The movement of any figure or figures to any part of the stage is then achieved with a clear order and not a series of conversations, explanations and contradictions.

Footed Screens—Folding Screens

We now turn to quite a different method of constructing and using a Background Setting. Our introduction to the subject in Section 1 gave us a fairly flexible, single screen method, but one limited merely to backing the acting-area. Our next step gave us a fuller surround to the acting-area but an arrangement limited to a fixed shape and size. In this section we shall combine the flexibility of our first simple screen setting with the complete surround of the side-hung arras setting, to give, possibly, the most useful branch of this Background type of setting.

For this, the curtains are divided into unit strips of a convenient width, generally from four to six feet, pleated, and each is hung on its own independent frame, which can be placed self-standing on its own special feet at any part of the stage. The combinations and arrangements of a set of eight or ten of these screens, coupled with certain details, are almost inexhaustible.

To begin with, by reducing the width of our unit frame from sixteen feet to something like four feet, we simplify the problem of its support. The frames of such a set need rarely be more than eight feet high. And the method of support is to provide each frame with its own feet. The frames may either be hung with curtains or canvassed and painted. This type of footed screen is suggested by several books on the theatre, but they rarely add that if the feet are not made to fold the problem of storing is immense; and they completely omit a point of the first importance, that, unless these feet are properly designed, with regard to one special point, the whole scheme will not work at all. Nobody has examined in print the construction of the units of a footed screen set. One may know of them without realizing their difficulties, and I am inclined to suppose that no set of screens has been made without considerable addition to the printed instructions. What will happen to some of these feet when the screens join

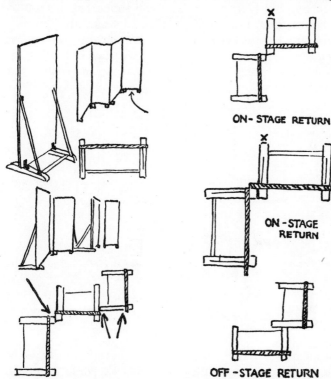

Fig. 87. *The primary difficulties of footed screens.*

Fig. 88. *The setting of footed screens at right angles, with a solution of the difficulty of the on-stage return, by in-setting the foot.*

at right angles? This matter requires looking into so that, once and for all, the difficulty is faced and removed. Because it has never been faced, this convenient method is seldom seen on the amateur stage. It is admirably suited to certain types of halls, especially those that have no proscenium and no facilities for hanging. Let us imagine such a footed screen and its grouping with others. Figs. 87 to 96 are almost self-explanatory. Taken together they show various modifications in a set of screens that upon assembly will at length avoid the primary difficulty of footed screens. In Fig. 87, taken alone, the difficulty is shown. At the top to the left is the back view of a screen, pin-hinged to a base and supported thereon by two braces, and, just beside, a plan in which the screen is shaded and the base left white. At the bottom, three screens are shown assembled at right angles, with arrows indicating the obstruction the feet present to joining the screens. In practice,

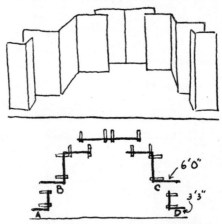

*Fig. 89. A set of footed screens with plan showing
the difficulty of the feet in the off-stage return.*

the appearance of the diagram on the top-right can never be attained. Instead we get the appearance shown in the group at the centre. (Note, in the top-right drawing, the arrow indicating the undesirable empty space below the screens through which the feet of the people behind may be seen.)

In Fig. 88, the first move to solve the difficulty of joining screens at an angle is made, by insetting one of the two feet on each screen. The top plan represents two screens upon the stage right, one up-and-down-stage, the other returning on-stage at its top edge. The arrangement presents a gap, but if the foot marked X is inset a few inches from the stage-right side of the screen, the two screens will join as shown in the centre plan.

66

So much for the 'on-stage return'. The 'off-stage return', shown in the lowest plan on Fig. 88, presents a greater difficulty. Let us consider it.

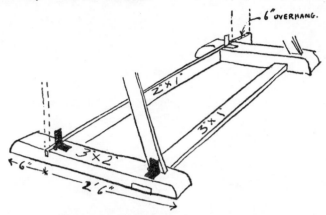

Fig. 90. Detailed construction of a normal foot.

In Fig. 89 is given a rough sketch of an arrangement of a full set of such screens; if we look at the plan below we see that the feet of all screens can be satisfactorily fitted together save those on screens A, B, C and D, whose feet would interfere with those of the screens set at right angles behind them.

Let us consider the construction of the feet of normal screens and then adapt the feet of A, B, C and D to suit that construction.

Fig. 90 gives the construction of the normal foot and explains itself.

Fig. 91 shows the back view of two screens at right angles, with the feet of the screen on our right specially adapted to fit over the normal feet of the other. One of its feet has been removed, as shown in Fig. 92 (viewed from the front).

Fig. 91. Solution of the difficulty of the off-stage return by means of a special foot.

It should be specially noticed that one of the braces is arranged to reach to a higher point up the back of the screen than the other, so as to allow the brace of the adjoining screen to reach underneath it as in Fig. 91.

Figs. 93 and 94 make this important point; that such a specially-footed screen may be used *either* up-and-down-stage on the stage-*right, or* on-and-off-stage on the stage-*left.* This

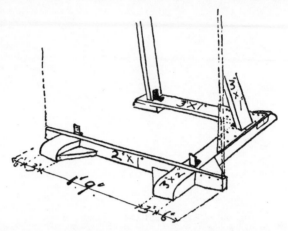

Fig. 92. Detailed construction of a special foot for narrow screens.

specially-footed screen is a narrow one measuring 3 ft. 3 in. wide. If, however, we turn to the wider 6 ft. screen then we can arrange a modification of the special foot as shown in Fig.

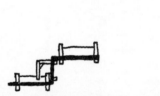

Fig. 93. Any given, narrow, special-footed screen may be used only up-and-down stage on one side of the stage, or see Fig. 94.

Fig. 94. A given, narrow, special-footed screen may be used only on-and-off stage on the other side of the stage.

95, by which it can be used in either position and on either side of the stage. Fig. 95 shows the construction and is viewed from the front. Fig. 96 shows the use of the specially-footed wide screen in plan—giving its arrangement in the two positions on the stage-right and in the two on the stage-left.

To turn now to the actual practice, we shall find that a typical store of footed screens might consist of a number of plain screens of various widths, together with (generally) an equal number of normal sets of feet and brace-pieces, stored

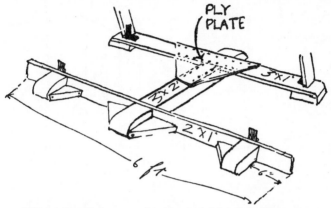

Fig. 95. Detailed construction of a special foot for wide screens.

separately and ready to be pin-hinged into place when needed for a show. In addition to the normal feet there would be at least two specially arranged wide feet (6 ft. each as in Fig. 95) and four specially-arranged narrow feet (3 ft. 3 in. as in Fig. 92) which would be used or not according to the demands of the particular set or group of sets then to be staged.

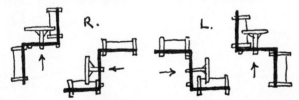

Fig. 96. A wide special-footed screen may be used in either position on either side of the stage.

The use of the screens may be supplemented with certain details, for instance a couple of small foliage set-pieces as in Fig. 97.

Perhaps the best way to describe the many potentialities of this style of setting (which is almost the only one possible in certain circumstances) would be to glance at a dozen or so imaginary special sets.

First, let me remind you again of the limited conditions under which we are still working at this early stage of our

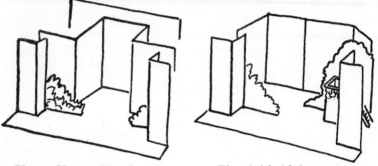

Fig. 97. The use of footed screens   *Fig. 98. (2) A balcony scene.*
(1) A simple garden.

study: we have no proscenium, nor can we as yet fit one up; we have no 'flies' and no possibility of hanging from above. We have no front curtain. Our conditions are a hall with seats and at one end an empty, simple platform.

Fig. 99. (3) An arbour scene.   *Fig. 100. (4) An interior scene.*

Fig. 98 shows an adaptation of Fig. 97 into a setting suitable for a balcony scene, with a rostrum on the stage left, and a balustrade upon it, with a high foliage set-piece to back it.

Fig. 99 is a simple presentation of an arbour scene with trees in tubs (either real or cut in profile) and a seat.

70

Fig. 100 is our first interior where the windows at the back are two painted sheets of ply on legs leaning against the screens. (Suppose them black windows with white or pale ochre bars and vermillion legs against a dull buff set of screens.) Two pedestals, one at either side in front, carry some detail characteristic of the room, and the fireplace is built of framed-up plywood sheets upon a wide hearth of floor-boards to which it is bracketed by a couple of purely decorative sweeping curves of ply arising from the hearth sides and curving up the sides of the fireplace. The

Fig. 101. (5) A temple, showing possible method of scene change.

mantelshelf would be a floor-board supported on angle-brackets. A last note to the set might be the suspension of two little silhouette portraits (or such like) hung either side from a cord. Notice that opposite the fireplace is an entrance with a backing. This is our first set that is not symmetrical.

In Fig. 101 we suppose a temple with a set-piece of the god at the back, and simple block seats arranged symmetrically.

But the great interest of Fig. 101 is that it introduces us to a method of scene change. At the end of the scene in the temple, suppose a stage-hand stationed behind each of the wing screens. The seats are taken away and the screens move forward as the arrows indicate and take up the arrangement shown in Fig. 102, and upon this set a front scene can now be played while the next scene is arranged behind. Now such a moving of the scenery, apparently by itself, and in full view of the audience can be very effectively and neatly done. As an idea, it again belongs to a centuries-old tradition, and is well in the spirit of the

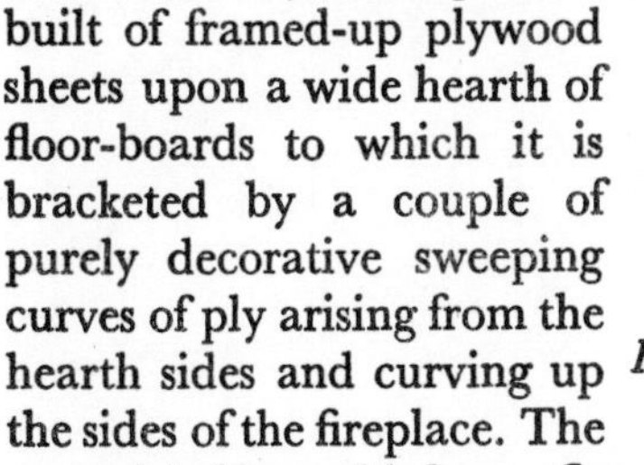

Fig. 102. (6) The setting of the screens during a scene change.

ingenious scene-changes of that Father of English scenery, Inigo Jones.

The movement of the scenery needs care and rehearsal and a great deal of shrewd planning beforehand, and a careful plot of movements must be made so that every single feature

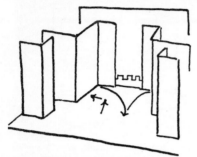

Fig. 103. (7) A rampart scene, show-ing method of opening and closing.

Fig. 104. (8) A cottage interior scene.

in the change (such as clearing a piece of furniture from the path of a screen) shall be part of the show and of its tempo—all smooth and well-drilled—and then it will be a pleasure to look at and an interest and a draw to all spectators.

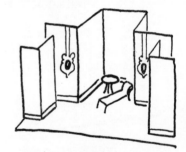

Fig. 105. (9) A small interior scene, occupying half the back with the next scene ready in the other half for dis-closure by sliding a screen across.

Fig. 106. (10) The stamping of a period atmosphere.

Fig. 102 might open to such a scene as Fig. 103 which might be a rampart for Hamlet or Macbeth. The arrows also suggest possibilities of scene-closing again.

Fig. 104 is a simple kitchen interior played in a narrowed

set, and Fig. 105, another simple interior, this time an office, in which only the right-hand half of the upper stage is used, and the scene-change is effected by lifting forward the back screen covering the left half of the set, and sliding it sideways to open the fresh half of the stage and to conceal the old. There is of course no reason in these cases to restrict the acting, or a piece of furniture that can be convincingly 'doubled' (or used in both scenes), to the small area within the scene at the back of the stage; after the scene has opened, the action can spread to the full width of the lower stage, retreating again at the close of the scene.

Fig. 107. (11) A conventionalized eavesdropping scene.

Fig. 106 shows the stamping of the character of a period interior by two pieces of furniture and, say, a couple of mirrors, decoratively framed (and faultlessly chosen), each screwed to a length of floorboard, painted a clear and relevant colour and hooked over the top of the screen. Notice that skirting-boards may be painted along the bottom of the screens. The flavour of any period can be just as simply attained by the application of one or two very well-chosen details upon the screens.

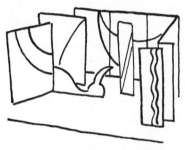

Fig. 108. (12) A conventionalized painted set.

Fig. 107 might be called a 'psychological' arrangement of screens, when for, let us say, a love-scene overlooked by a group of eavesdroppers, the unknowing couple play on a striped couch, while from the edge of each of the diagonal flats behind, pops the head of an eavesdropper, all appearing and withdrawing in unison.

You see the footed screen form is not limited to one type of show, and Fig. 108 shows that there are possibilities even of 'expressionistic' styles in the form, and of a good deal of painted decoration, provided that the decoration is flat pattern and non-representational.

Remember, these screens are not 'scenery', they are pieces of theatre.

Generally speaking, avoid doors and arches, as not in the terms of the medium, and if you must close your entrances, work on the principle of the gate.

To make our review complete we should note in passing the use of sets of ordinary two-fold screens; though generally speaking any rearrangement during the show is impossible without dropping a front curtain.

The Full Folding Screen Set differs from the first simple screen I described in that it provides sides as well as background, and completely embraces the acting-area. It is more flexible than the side-hung curtain set, and needs less elaborate carpentry than the footed screen set, though it is not capable of so many variations.

But it is mentioned in all books on simple scenery, in fact it is so well described that I cannot do better than name Marjorie Somerscales' book on *The Improvised Stage* and refer you for details to her.

The elements of the Somerscales screen sets are very simple. They consist of a backcloth and four double-leaved screens with reversible hinges. On one side the screens are painted green, and on the other they are natural hessian, and they are occasionally used in conjunction with a simple side-hung traverse curtain, thereby allowing change of the back pair of screens during the show. To these essential elements are added certain painted details, which, together with the traverse curtain, suggest that this type of setting is rather in the nature of an extensive proscenium, in a small opening in the back of which the scenery proper is concentrated in the way we found typical of the ancient theatre tradition.

For this reason the handling of these screens as described by

Miss Somerscales rather overlaps from the pure background section into that which I have still to describe as possibly the most useful and widely adaptable of all—'Detail' Setting.

But for pure Detail Setting a proscenium is necessary, and I think in most cases the arrangements of the screens by Miss Somerscales are with a proscenium frame in mind. They are, nevertheless, suggestive of possibilities for the bare proscenium-less platform, which we are still considering.

Another system of screen setting, designed by Mr. H. Weston Wells, was printed in *Drama* and reprinted in a pamphlet by the National Federation of Women's Institutes, 39 Eccleston Street, S.W. 1. The pamphlet contains diagrams and a page of descriptive text, also a list of interesting plays, and costs threepence. I think that certain original contributions would have to be made by anyone building this set to suit his own special conditions, for the comments upon it are very brief in the pamphlet, and one would have been interested to have had more detail; still, at its price, you could not wish for a better nucleus for that private collection of methods of setting that should be the ever-growing possession of every company of players.

SECTION 6

The Lighting of Background Sets

Whether the lighting of the various types of Background Setting is effected under good conditions with suitable special apparatus, or under bad conditions with the existing lighting apparatus of the hall itself, the principle behind the use of the lights is the same.

It is the principle of out-door flood-lighting.

First, one or two notes as to the details. Two types of lanterns are used, the first a simple box, open at one side, with the lamp inside and a reflector at the back of it to throw the flood of light from which the lantern gets its name of 'flood lantern'. The second is a lantern generally cylindrical, with a lamp inside and a concave mirror reflector behind it at one end of the cylinder, and a lens at the other which concentrates the scattering rays into a directable beam, whose pool of light when thrown on an object has the sharp circular edge of a spot, which spot can be increased or decreased in area by moving the position of the lamp and reflector in the lantern with regard to the lens. This is the 'spot' lantern, or focussing lantern.

The point to remember is that the first, the flood, splashes a wide uncontrolled flood of light, and the second, the spot, a controlled beam with which a given spot can be picked out.

In practice, this method of lighting reduces itself to the one ingenuity of the right placing of the lanterns.

As a rule the Floods should be on the ground or stage level, lighting the *scenery* upwards from the front, and the Spots should be above the heads of the first rows of stalls, lighting the *actors* obliquely downwards, or at the side of the hall, lighting the actors obliquely sideways. The circular pools of

76

light they throw should in general fall upon the stage floor at places where the actor is situated at important moments of the presentation, but (again, I remind you, generally speaking) the spot should not fall on the scenery. The lighting of the scenery should be left to the flood lanterns.

Rarely, in certain circumstances, the flood lights may be directly over the acting area, lighting downwards, and so illuminating stage and actors, but here, they are in full view of the audience, who must be carefully screened from seeing the brilliant and distracting dazzle of the interior of the lamp itself.

Ideally, lighting from above should not be used unless there are borders with which to mask the lights, and that would take us into another section of our story and another style of setting.

In a circus where the audience sit on all sides of the 'stage', which is the arena, the lighting is from arena-floods, provided with special cowls so as to restrict their field of light to the arena itself and allow none to fall directly into the eyes of the audience. With equal care they may occasionally be used over our Background Set, when the existing light-pendants cannot be supplemented, but great care should be taken in cowling them.

The most satisfactory method remains the lighting from the front below, by floods; from the sides across by spots, and occasionally floods; and from above and in front, backwards and downwards almost always by spots.

It is not my intention to deal with the technique of lighting in any detail but I would point out to you the value of home-made lanterns carefully placed and fed by flexes from the existing light-points, about whose construction full and expert details are given in Harold Ridge's book *Stage Lighting* (2nd ed., Heffer).

I will here only emphasize the importance of making careful calculation of the currents which the dimensions of the existing cables and any added flexes will pass with safety and of making specially certain not to overload. There is no other way to insure this than by simple calculations based on voltages, and on the dimensions and resistances of cables, and for these I refer you to the specialist, Harold Ridge.

But this point is important here: the point of using your lamps, not for a vague general illumination in the way too often employed in the lighting of the rooms of our homes to-day, but as sources of directed light, each placed with judgment and experiment, and very closely on the principle of the expert flood-lighting of civic architecture, where every lamp must make its effect on the surface it lights.

Move your lanterns to places that will be effective. Institute and enjoy lighting-rehearsals and watch for any interesting effects of lights and shadows, of concentration or direction of beams, and seize on such of them as help your show, while you store in your mind for further use all the others that attract you.

You will learn thereby more than several who pride themselves on their knowledge of lighting, for you will have had an unparalleled apprenticeship in the art of *placing* your lights, since that is too often forgotten or ignored when an equipped stage is at one's disposal, and one is inclined to switch on the lights in their places, forgetting to direct them.

CHAPTER TWO

The Proscenium comes into the Story

SECTION 7

The Fourth Wall—Curtain Fit-ups supplying their own Proscenium

We now reach a point of transition. We must go from the more or less simple *background* to the beginnings of the *full surround* for our acting-area. That is to say we have now to turn and take a point of view where our acting-area is no longer a fragment of a larger indefinite area, particularized by a *background* at its farther limit, but instead is a much more sharply isolated space, limited on four sides and above as is the floor of a box.

Not only have we to consider in this full surround the back wall and the two side walls, but also, for the first time, the 'ceiling' and the 'fourth wall'. The Fourth Wall is generally defined as a completely imaginary wall situated at the foot-lights and dividing the audience from the stage. Especially has this conception of the imaginary 'fourth wall' been stressed by those who look upon the stage as the usual seat of a square box-set or room-interior—and a realistic room at that. Because of the stress of the realists on their pet phrase and their adjective 'imaginary', it seems gradually to be slipping from notice that there is in fact a fourth wall to a stage, and a very actual wall at that. And it makes little difference to the reality of this wall that its central area is knocked away to form the opening through which we see the stage. There remain, only too definitely, the areas of the wall around the opening, and they come to have possibly the mos effectual influence upon the planning of our settings of anything in the whole theatre.

Just how far that influence goes and to what scientific means we must resort to cope with it we are not ready to discuss in full at the moment. It is sufficient that the very real remnants of this fourth wall bring us again to that factor we found in another form earlier on—the Proscenium Opening or Arch.

The other important direction in which we must now look is upward, at the management of that 'ceiling' or other masking device at the top of our set behind the arch. For the moment we will consider this in its simplest form as an arrangement of *stage borders* and *proscenium border* and discuss the actual fitting of these to the kind of background set we have described, so as to make of the set, for the first time, a 'Full Surround Setting' instead of a 'Background Setting'—a setting that masks in all directions, presents no holes through which you can glimpse the beyond, and, viewed from any seat whatever in the house, is a neat and tight nest within the proscenium opening.

Before we go on to consider ways of making the proscenium arch a fixed feature of the theatre-building, with the setting a distinct entity behind it (which carries us out of the range of the simple hall, with its bare platform, and begins to lead us into the territory of the equipped theatre) there are two types of setting which serve as a very good transition. They are forms of self-standing curtain settings which provide their own proscenium.

The first is described by Rodney Bennett in an elementary, but refreshingly vivid section on scenery in his book *Let's do a Play!* Mr. Bennett treats scenery rather as a game than as a craft, but I have certainly no wish to quarrel with that. I should only have liked a fuller treatment, perhaps, of certain technical difficulties.

Mr. Bennett's diagram shows a temporary stage built upon trestles. The stage is in four 10 ft. × 5 ft. sections (which it seems to me would be enormously heavy to move) and is furnished with four columns of wood, braced upright to support an overhead framework of some elaboration, from which a full curtain set may be hung with either 'straight' or 'wing' sides.

Turning from play to work, from the amateur's stage to the professional's, we find, constructed on a similar principle, what is perhaps one of the most interesting self-contained full fit-up systems that can be found. It is the system evolved by the Arts' League of Service Travelling Theatre. This company works in conditions very like those of the travelling players of old, save that their complete equipment has to go into a small motor-lorry and not a cart.

The requirements which the system of setting they have evolved fulfils are these: It must be capable of being set up anywhere, with no assistance whatever from any outside agent, save the surface of the platform it stands on. It must provide its own proscenium and front curtain. It must supply borders and a means of hanging them. It must be capable of wing sides or straight sides. Furthermore, and these are hard

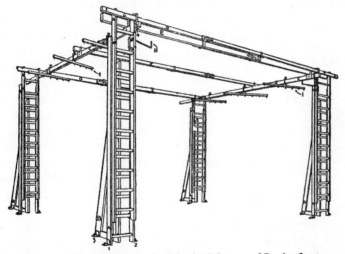

Fig. 109. The old framework of the Arts' League of Service fit-up.
(Courtesy of Arts' League of Service).

conditions, it must not only be capable of packing into small space on the lorry that conveys the costumes and properties, but it must be capable of fitting halls of very different size; it must be extensible and contractable in all directions, in height, in width and in depth.

I am able to show, by the courtesy of the Arts' League of Service, not only their early scheme of fit-up but, for comparison, a new form made in steel tubes to which the natural development of things has led them to-day. For each of these fit-ups, the old and the new, I give the company's own drawings and a description in the company's own words. The first wooden fit-up is shown in Fig. 109; here is the description:

'The whole of the structure is supported on the four adjustable ladders (A). These are held upright by strong wooden braces (B) which are fastened to the ladders at three points by means of hinges and pins. The ladders are then screwed into the floor with screw-eyes or hand-screws at points 1, 2 and 3.

'The battens, like the ladders, are all adjustable and may be expanded or contracted as the size of the stage requires. The side battens (C) are the first to be fixed in position and

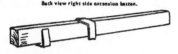

Back view right side extension batten.

Fig, 109a. Detail of fit-up.
(*Courtesy of Arts' League of Service.*)

are hung on iron brackets fixed on the inner sides of the ladders a little below the top. These should not be allowed to project more than 1 inch in advance of the front brackets, otherwise the masking material will be disturbed. A screw should therefore be driven into the batten at point 4 to avoid risk of the batten being pulled out of the bracket. The battens may, however, project as far as is convenient behind the back ladders, when the rear points will form an excellent structure on which to hang a sky cloth behind the back curtains should this be necessary. The front and back battens (D and G) are hung in brackets fixed to the front of the ladders and immediately above the side battens. Batten E is heavier than the others and carries the "tabs" or front working curtains. It hangs in iron sockets which are screwed to the side battens about 3 inches behind the front ladders. Batten F is supported in a similar manner and carries a flood light.

'The Z irons (H) are carried in sockets on the front ladders and support two small curtains for masking the prompt and O.P. corners. The theatre also carries two small extension battens (Fig. 109a) which support the side masking curtains. They are fixed by means of two iron hooks over and under the front batten (D, Fig. 109) at points 5 and 6, and 7 and 8.

'The stage curtains are hung on light swivel-battens which are clamped into the main structure as shown in Fig. 109. These light[1] battens also continue along the back but have been omitted in the drawing to avoid congestion. By means of these swivels the light battens can be used either parallel with or at right angles to the side battens (C) giving free exit and entrance or boxing in the stage as the scene requires.

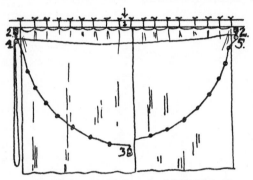

I Centre of batten E. 2. Sections of battens C. 3. Sand-bag or lead weight to ensure quick and efficient closing.
4. A twin pulley block. 5. A single pulley block.

Fig. 109b. Detail of Tabs in A.L.S. fit-up.
(Courtesy of Arts' League of Service.)

'Should a window or a door be necessary, it is set in place of one strip of material which can be neatly rolled up and fastened with drawing-pins along the top of the door, the two curtains on either side covering the ends of the roll and being correspondingly pinned down the sides of the door-frame to the floor. A neater effect can be obtained if there is sufficient time for the change by removing the strip of material: a shorter strip is then hung on the swivel batten reaching only to the top of the door (in case of a window, a further piece is hung from the bottom of the window frame to the floor). The door or window is held in position by light expanding battens which hook over the main structure and are bolted to the window or door frame. A door should be secured on the floor in the same way as the ladders.

[1]Meaning 'light in weight', not battens for lamps.—R.S.

85

'The working curtains are tied on to batten E with tapes allowing an overlap in the centre to insure proper closing. They are rigged as shown in Fig. 109*b* and controlled from the prompt side.

'The borders are stretched on strings tied to battens C. They are about 18 inches deep and their number and position must be determined by the line of sight, which will vary according to the proportions of the theatre.

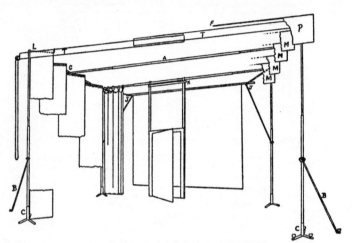

Fig. 109c. The new steel A.L.S. fit-up.
(*Courtesy of Arts' League of Service.*)

'The front border and side masking curtains are stretched on to batten D and the ladders with drawing-pins.

'The structure is adaptable in other ways which will be found by experience when in use.'

For some companies the making of a steel fit-up such as the following will be more difficult than that of the old, for the parts need a good deal of preparation in a workshop which would be beyond the scope of some amateur carpenters who could tackle the wooden scheme with confidence. But the steel is lighter, as flexible and more compact than the wood and it seems to be the method of the future, at any rate for

this particular company. It is illustrated in Figs. 109c and
109d and is described as follows:

'The new A.L.S. fit-up theatre was built according to the
League's design by the Hall Manufacturing Co., Ltd. It is
made of telescopic steel tubes which are more adaptable,
lighter in weight, less in bulk and can be handled with
greater ease than the wooden structure of the past. To this is
added the advantage of a curtain track which allows for

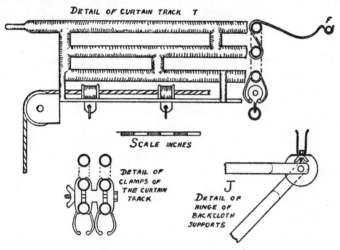

Fig. 109d. Details of steel fit-up.
(Courtesy of Arts' League of Service.)

smooth working. The back curtains are on rings so that they
can be opened or closed with ease.

'The main telescopic steel tubes can be clamped to any
desired length within their range, i.e. 8 to 14 feet on the upright tubes, and 9 to 16 feet on the horizontals.

'The curtain track which forms the front of the structure is
of built-up steel (see Fig. 109d) and is adjustable from 12 to
20 feet, along which the front curtains run.

'The thin steel rod (F) which carries the pelmet (P) is a
separate unit, supported by brackets on the front of the track.
This also carries the two lengths of material which mask the
uprights and form the side frames of the proscenium.

'To erect the fit-up the curtain track is laid on the stage and clamped to the desired width. Next the uprights are fitted to the track and adjusted to the height required. Two men can then lift the complete section, fit the ends of the uprights into the stands (C) which are then screwed to the floor, the whole front section being steadied by adjustable braces (B) which are also screwed to the floor. The three tubes forming the back section are then dealt with in the same way, except that the back curtains, which are on large rings, are threaded on to the horizontal rod before erecting. Two small L-shaped irons (L) are fitted to the heads of the front uprights. These carry two strips of masking for the prompt and o.p. corners and serve to mask the flood lights. The side horizontal tubes (G) are then fitted on to the top of the front and back uprights and wing nuts clamp the structure.

'A centre rod (A) which fits on to the two side tubes braces the structure outwards. This is also utilized to carry the Sunray flood which lights the stage from above. The side curtains of the set are hung on short pieces of wood, fixed with swivel fittings to the side tubes. They can be opened to give a free entrance—yet mask the wings—or closed if a box set is required.

'The top of the structure is masked with borders (M) stretched across the set with cords. If any extra masking is required to extend from the proscenium sides of the structure this is carried by two telescopic wooden battens fixed to the ends of the curtain track (T).

'The back, or sky cloth, is fastened to a batten and dropped into two brackets (J) which are fixed to the back uprights.

'When a door or window piece is used it is clamped to two extendable wooden battens that hook over the back horizontal rod. The back curtains are pulled aside and the space above the door or window is filled in with a piece of the same material as the curtains. This is neatly pulled over a light cross batten (K) at the top and fixed with drawing pins (H). This forms a unit which can be built beforehand, set and removed with ease.

'The whole structure can be rapidly dismantled, and will be found of great use in village halls with limited storage space. It can also be erected in any good sized room by reason of its adaptability.'

Further to this scheme, I might point those who are interested to what seem promising possibilities in the 'Ang-Kary Coupler'. This is a unit similar to but slightly lighter than those one sees holding each intersection of steel-tube scaffolding. It is designed to take any $\frac{3}{4}$ in. diameter tube or rod of wood or of metal—especially electric cable conduit. No threading of the tube-ends is needed, but full-sized frameworks of considerable complexity and reasonable strength may be built with tubes and couplers much as one uses the strips and nuts in a meccano outfit. So far as I know, the possibilities of the coupler for metal fit-ups have never been explored. Those interested can obtain a profusely illustrated pamphlet of its uses from the manufacturers, the Dudley Foundry Co. Ltd., Moor Lane Foundry, Brierly Hill, Staffs. The couplers cost 8s. per two dozen. But experimenters must make their own plans and tests. I should be interested to hear their results.

Let me add, in conclusion, that the self-standing guy-rope fit-up in Fig. 77 could be provided, like those just discussed, with its own proscenium border on the down-stage wire, and a stage-border on a light batten clipped across from side-wire to side-wire.

SECTION 8

The Construction of a Separate Proscenium Arch— The Simplest Proscenium—A Built-in Proscenium—A Temporary Proscenium

We have now to consider the design and building of a separate proscenium arch for temporary or permanent use in a hall. There are three possible kinds of proscenium:

1. The simplest arrangement for a small hall, capable of being put up with the fewest fixtures to the walls.

2. A more elaborate arrangement that should be built to stand more or less permanently, and would *either* convert the

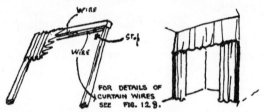

Fig. 110. A simple proscenium, front view and detail.

hall into a theatre with the beginnings of theatrical equipment, and drive as few fixtures in the original structure as possible. *Or* would mask a stage whose walls and roof were available for as many fixtures of stage mechanism as were needed.

3. A removable proscenium, capable of being taken away or put up when needed, and as easily stored as ordinary stage scenery when not in use.

For the first and last of these three alternative needs, I can supply a straightforward arrangement in detail. But for the second, where the proscenium is a more or less permanent part of the building, its construction must depend in detail upon the hall itself and I can give only a skeleton suggestion

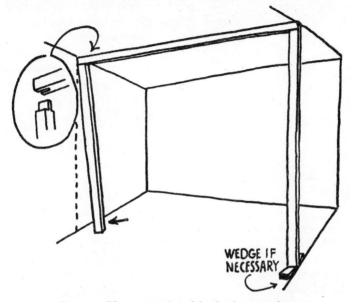

Fig. 111. The construction of the simple proscenium.

and leave the carpenter to adapt such of it as is useful in the circumstances to his own particular plans.

The simplest proscenium arrangement you can put up consists of three pieces of timber and a front curtain with its pelmet or valance (Fig. 110).

The timber is 3 in. × 2 in., one piece is as long as the ceiling is wide and goes across the top, the other two are as long as the room is high, and are tenoned into the ends of the cross-piece, and stand against the walls to support it. The timber is, of course, used edgeways, that is, with the 2 in. side against the wall and the 3 in. projecting into the room (Fig. 111).

Fig. 112. Supporting blocks for a simple proscenium.

Fig. 112 shows four blocks screwed permanently into the wall and painted in with the decoration of the room, between which each of the uprights

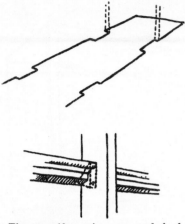

may be fixed, and Fig. 113 shows the help that may be derived from a picture rail from which a section has been cut just wide enough to take the upright—alternatively, if cutting the picture-rail is not practicable, how the upright itself may be cut to fit round the rail, blocks (indicated by dotted lines) being screwed to the rail on either side of the upright. Above is the plan of a room with pilasters, or breaks-forward in the walls which can be used to nest the uprights of the proscenium against.

Fig. 113. Alternative supports derived from a picture-rail or from a set-forward in the wall.

Let us look now at a proscenium to suit the second set of circumstances, when it is to be built as a more or less permanent part of the hall. Here, as I said, final details depend on the hall itself, and what I offer are merely suggestions, some of which may be adaptable to a given set of circumstances. We are considering a system by which extensions from the back of the proscenium, across the ceiling, to the back wall of the stage may be designed to serve as a support for scenery upon the stage.

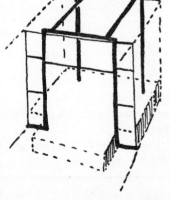

Fig. 114. Main principle of a built-in proscenium provided with two overhead bearers for scenery.

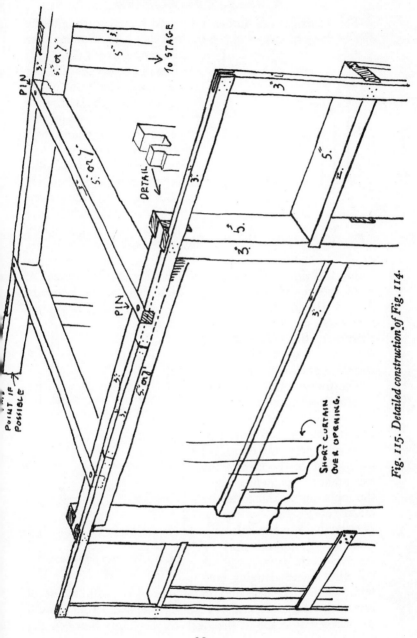

Fig. 115. Detailed construction of Fig. 114.

93

The dimensions of timber to be used vary according to the size of the job, from 3 in. × 2 in. to 5 in. × 3 in. or more. The

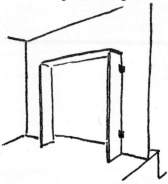

whole arrangement (Fig. 114) consists of two arches of heavy wood, one at the front of the stage and one at the back, with two overhead bearers joining their tops, to act as beams from which to hang the scenery.

Fig. 115 shows the detailed construction with indication of the joints used and the dimensions of wood. The whole is of such a size that it fits tightly into the end of the hall, the sides of the front against the

Fig. 116. Proscenium 'thickness-pieces' viewed from behind.

walls, and the cross-bearers against the ceiling. If a block of wood is screwed firmly into the side walls of the house in front of the top batten across the back of the stage, the rigidity of the whole will be assured, even if the wood shrinks slightly with age.

The framework of the proscenium front itself is made of 3 in. × 1 in. on the lines of the simple framing of our first piece of scenery, and is applied to the face of the first of the two arches. It is useful to give the opening a thickness by means of 'reveals' as shown from the back in Fig. 116.

Such a framework may be covered with one of four materials—with hanging cur-

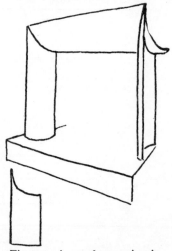

Fig. 117. A curved proscenium in Ensoflex.

tains; with stretched and painted canvas; with sheets of plywood, when the battens forming the framework should be planned to come at the back of the joints between the

sheets of ply, so that the edges of ply can be nailed
to them all the way round; and lastly, with a material
whose mention here is only to be taken as a suggestion, for it
is a new material only recently marketed and still remains to

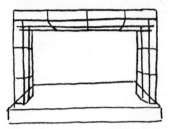

Fig. 118. Cage-framework for Fig. 117.

be tested in stage use. Its name is Ensoflex and it is a sort of
tough, slightly-ribbed, fibrous cardboard. It is said to be very
durable and its great features are its astonishing flexibility,
and the large size of the pieces in which it can be bought—up

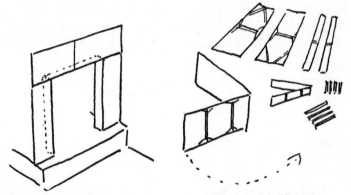

Fig. 119. (1) A removable pro-   *Fig. 120. (2) The parts.*
scenium.

to 10 ft. wide by 75 ft. long. The possibilities of Ensoflex for
building scenery seem great and well worth trying.

A special suggestion for its use on a proscenium (based on
its flexibility) is made in Figs. 117 and 118 where, in Fig. 118,
is a simple cage of battens, nailed together, and in Fig. 117, a
curved proscenium made of sheets of Ensoflex bent round and

nailed to the battens. The proscenium top is bent from a rectangular piece, and the sides cut to the shape shown below.

A third form of proscenium arch which can be put up or taken away when needed is shown in Fig. 119. It consists of

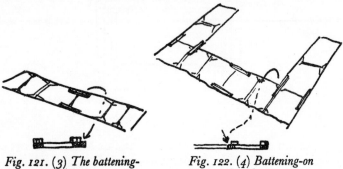

Fig. *121.* (*3*) *The battening-
out of the top.*

Fig. *122.* (*4*) *Battening-on
the sides.*

two sides, a top in two parts hinged together, three reveals (the longest reveal may need to be hinged in the centre for transport), and eight lengths of 3 in. × 1 in. for battening out (Fig. 120). The main parts are made like the simple screen

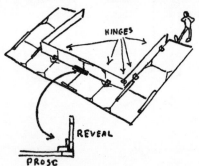

Fig. *123.* (*5*) *Adding the thickness-pieces.*

with which we began, or better, on the principle of the flat proper. I shall concern myself here chiefly with assembly and erection.

In Fig. 121 the hinged top-piece is brought upon the stage, unfolded and laid face downwards. (Let us watch from the corner of the dress-circle.) The join is then 'battened-out' (in the way that was used to fasten the top extension to our first piece of scenery in default of plugs and sockets) and it is especially to be noted that, as indicated by the arrow in the little section, what is to be the lower of the two battens (the more distant just now) is set an inch in from the edge of the frames, so as to leave room for the reveal later. Next the sides are assembled (Fig. 122) and the joins similarly battened-out,

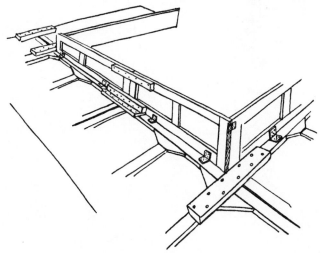

Fig. 124. (6) Bird's-eye view from corner of circle of assembled proscenium lying face down on the stage.

for which purpose it should be seen that the outer toggle-rails (or cross-rails) of the two top flats be arranged to come directly in a line with the inner stiles of the side flats. Here again provision has to be made for the fixing of the reveals by placing the inner of the pair of battens an inch away from the side of the opening.

Next the top reveal is battened-out, with the same pre-caution taken about in-setting the down-stage batten, and it is fitted in place with pin-hinges as in Fig. 123, where the small section shows the fitting of the reveal against the back of the top of the opening. The side reveals are then pin-hinged in place and are so arranged that the top reveal rests upon their tops, and is fixed thereto by another pin-hinge. If we viewed that part of the proceedings shown in Fig. 123, with opera-glasses from our perch, Fig. 124 gives a rough idea of the details we should see.

One of the stage-hands in Fig. 123 is standing with his foot against the bottom of the proscenium. He is waiting there,

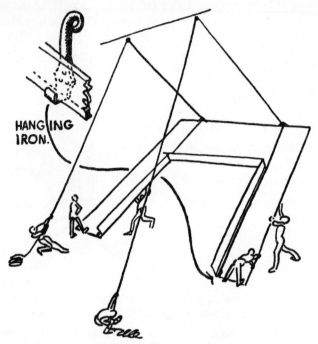

Fig. 125. (7) Details of erecting.

with a purpose, for the erection of the piece, which is effected as follows:

A 'bridle' or 'grummet' is nailed to either side of the top edge vertically above the sides of the opening. The grummet is simply a foot or so of sash-cord secured at either end with nails into the wood, at points about eight inches apart, so that it is not stretched but bent and loose.

A couple of lines are let down from pulleys in the ceiling, led through these grummets, and taken to the bottom of the proscenium sides, where they are made off to screw-eyes or hanging-irons.

Fig. 125 shows these lines being tightened and the whole thing being gradually drawn upright. (We are looking now from the stage side.) Note well the two men 'footing' the base, and the two 'walking' their hands down the proscenium as it goes up, supporting it with the greatest of care to relieve the battened joints of this great momentary bending strain, that they are not intended to bear. In Fig. 126 the man on the left at the foot, is taking the precaution to push

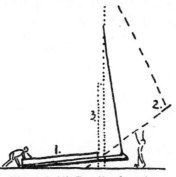

Fig. 126. (8) Details of erecting.

that foot forward as the proscenium is pulled up from position 1 to position 2, so that its base is increasingly brought near to the point it will occupy when in position 3, directly beneath the pulleys. In position 2 his mate is doing all he can to relieve the bending strain as the piece goes upright.

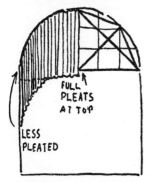

Fig. 127. Filling-in to the roof above a proscenium.

If such a proscenium is erected in a very high hall with a curved roof (like our old friend in Fig. 1), one of the arrangements suggested in Fig. 127 must be adopted to mask-in the top. To your left of Fig. 127, a curtain is hung from the roof itself; to the right, the existing rafters or tie-beams have been supplemented by battens which are to be covered with sheets of plywood. If the proscenium itself is to be made of curtain, the method on the left can be used and it is to be left to the taste of the designer whether the descending end of the curtain in the figure is to be cut off level with the edge at the centre, or left as part of the draping. In either case he must note that to ensure equal gathering the curtain-border must be pleated less at the side than at the centre, in increasing ratio as he goes out from that centre, because the horizontal distance apart of the fixings is virtually decreased by reason of the curvature of the ceiling.

SECTION 9

The Etiquette of the Front Curtain

Now that we have set a wall between the stage-world and the public, we have to consider a door for the opening in that wall, by which the public can be completely shut out when what we have to show them is not ready.

So we come to the Front Curtains or Drop. In the language of the theatre, the means of closing this opening is called 'Tabs' when it is of curtain, and generally a 'Drop' when it is a painted cloth.

The use of the word Tabs is a little loose, for originally, it seems, it applied in its full form of 'the Tableau Curtains' to that pair of curtains which parted in the centre and bunched sideways and upwards to drape the top corners of the proscenium opening, and disclosed the tableaux arranged on the stage at the conclusion of each scene in the old melodrama days

In our day, 'Tabs' is used indiscriminately for any form of proscenium curtain, either the sort I have just mentioned, or the side-drawing curtains that run on a railway, or the complete single curtain that ascends entire in its folds vertically into the flies.

Before we go into details of the hanging and working of tabs, there are certain facts to be pointed out. The first of these is: To drop the tabs is to break the atmosphere of the show. My concern in Theatre is primarily with presentation, with putting the show on. And this fact of breaking the atmosphere is of great importance to showmanship or the art of theatrical presentation.

An audience can be compared with a soldering-iron. When the show is on, the iron is in the fire and hot enough to effect that fusion which is the cementing of ideas and the fixing in people's minds of the point you make, but once remove your iron from the fire, or deprive the audience of the atmosphere of the show, and it becomes colder and less capable of that fusion with each succeeding second.

Obviously a careful solderer will not use his iron too hot, so that sometimes you may see him take it from the fire, hold it a few inches from his cheek to test it, and then, if it is too hot, wave it in the air for a moment before applying it to the work. So with your audience. After a special scene where the excitement is raised almost to fever-pitch, it may be that a moment's 'fanning' is of vital importance before the next scene is offered for their consideration.

But the timing of that interval needs the most delicate judgment. Let them cool too far and the opening of your next scene will be flat and your actors will have to do their work all over again. After an unduly long interval, in fact, the audience return to their seats from the distractions of conversation in bar or foyer, in that state of mind which says 'Ah, now, where were we?' And though they may not clearly realize it they may never grasp the situations of the play because of these interval distractions, and they criticize the show as men who have only seen half of it.

Intervals between the scenes of a play are late innovations in theatre history. They seem to have arisen as a poor expedient to which managers resorted for relief from the embarrassment created by more and more complicated sets of scenery that, because of the competition of other spectacle-purveyors, became more and more realistic in detail and more and more difficult to strike and set.

In the early days of scenery (which are no further back than the seventeenth century) this problem was handled differently. In his *Development of the Theatre*, Professor Allardyce Nicoll observes, 'Much as these Renascence theorists experimented' (with methods to make scenery easily changeable) 'it is surprising to note how they, and their successors, failed to realize the opportunities which a front curtain offered to an ambitious machinist and manager.'

For the front curtain in those days was only used at the beginning of a show to disclose, on a sudden, a brilliant stage to an assembled audience, and, at the end of the show, to veil the picture and signify the séance was broken and the performance over.

But we cannot share in Professor Nicoll's surprise that the machinist refrained from using the front curtain to veil the stage while he changed the scene. Rather would the really 'ambitious' machinist consider his design of poor ingenuity if the scenes could not be changed or 'transformed' as part of the show in full sight of the audience, adding thereby to its interest and spectacle instead of dropping the atmosphere and leaving the audience cold and flat—while perspiring stage-hands behind the curtain laboured to reduce this interval to the shortest space that could be arranged for such an evil.

No; the Renaissance machinist was far too good a man of the theatre to resort to the base expedient of breaking the show in pieces because his contrivance of the spectacle was too cumbrous and unimaginative to change without being hidden.

To-day when convention and liquor-licenses force intervals on a grudging producer, the cry goes up, and is often repeated, that long intervals are bad.

If it is humanly possible, the producer seeks (except for those inevitable inter-act breaks that are part of the theatre's contract) to compress each interval between scenes, so that the lights need not be put up in the auditorium. He knows very well that if that is to be avoided, the interval must be very short, for an audience becomes restive and may jeer if you leave it too long in the dark; the impression it receives of poor management behind the scenes may be too strong for the actors to live down when the curtain at length goes up.

To put up the lights for a short interval is an equal evil, for the concentration of the spectators is broken and they immediately begin to talk, to look around, to leave their seats. . . . If the play has been holding them, they resent the sudden dragging back to earth. If it has not yet succeeded in engaging their whole attention, they may rise and wander about after their own devices. Expecting—maybe hoping for—the usual long interval of a quarter of an hour, they are suddenly caught in the gangways and passages by darkness, and have to struggle back to their seats between the eyes of their less restless fellows and the bright stage upon which the curtain has suddenly gone up. There must follow disturbances in the audience, alarums and apologies to say the least of it, and such things are appallingly detrimental to the acting and the show.

There have been presenters who have ruined their show simply because they hadn't the showmanship to arrange for intelligent intervals. So you see, this curtain in the proscenium opening is potentially one of the greatest dangers to good presentation.

It is with the deepest feelings of amazement and disgust that we watch, sometimes, the treatment of the curtain in amateur and even professional presentations. It may be vigorously kicked from behind by a struggling stage-hand, so that you receive the impression that the show is nearly beyond the resources of the staff. Dignity is lost. Or the curtain may be thrust out in successive billows as someone walks across the stage, avoiding, one supposes, the newly-laid carpet, and an impression of the casualness of the staff remains clear in one's mind. Or the curtain is, with the grossest effrontery, plucked aside and the audience is inspected calmly by the eyes of some stripling in the cast, curious to see if any of his acquaintance is in the house.

Let me emphasize that such behaviour is bad, only because and when it is contrary to the atmosphere of the show produced. There are certain occasions of farce where such treatment may be amusing. When it is mere thoughtlessness, it is, at once, a desolating exposure of the company's level in theatre—a level so low as to paralyse one's sympathy, however one may seek to extend it.

There is a further point about this front curtain which may be of the subtlest value to a show, or may make just as subtle mischief if overlooked or bungled. This is the right handling of the curtain, and most of all the *timing* of the curtain, as it falls on a scene.

Here is a point of which the non-critical mind rarely sees the importance. He will sit back as the lights go up and say,

'My! that was a fine scene!' And that is all you want him to say. It may none the less be true that what contributed the final touch to his enthusiasm was a faultlessly-timed curtain closing at exactly the right speed, and to a heart's beat at exactly the right moment.

I remember vividly seeing a performance with a perfect curtain by a company of cotton-spinners. The play was *The Master of the House*. Throughout the scene, an Old Man had sat in a chair with his back to the audience, never speaking a word. A young man railed against him and shouted, 'I will be the Master of the House.' The Old Man died in the violence of the Young Man's speech. They covered him with a sheet. The room emptied save for these two. Then the Young Man's aggression failed; he began to go; he spoke his last line. He looked round the room, turned his back on the figure, went to the door and switched out the light. He opened the door, went out and closed it behind him. . . .

Then the curtain fell.

It was perhaps only a split second behind the ordinary unintelligent moment anybody might have chosen. But in that split second, there was suddenly conveyed the tragic realization who was still the 'Master of the House'!

There is no more subtle means of working on the feeling of an audience than by timing—by speed and pause—by sound and then silence. By a conclusion, and then—a full-stop.

We need to consider the working of front curtains with some idea of the dangers we have to avoid, and the effects we wish to make with them.

SECTION 10

The Working of the Front Curtain

In Fig. 128 is what is probably the most general form of tabs arrangement. It consists of a heavy batten, perhaps 5 in. × 2 in., on one of the narrow sides of which are fixed two wires with strainers. The ends of the wires are attached by means of large staples (C) driven into the wood. The wires overlap in the centre (see A, which is a plan of the batten,

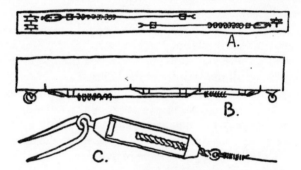

Fig. 128. Details of a simple curtain railway without the
working lines.

looking up). At one end of the batten is a double pulley, at the other a single. Looked at from the side (B), it will be seen that small blocks of wood are lodged in between the wires and the batten, near either end of each wire, as distance-pieces, serving to keep the wire free of the batten so as to allow the rings to run. The line by which the curtain is worked (Fig. 129) is an endless line led up (*a*) through one of the double pulleys, across to the single pulley, back to the second wheel of the double pulley (*b*), and down to the stage, where it is as

106

well to run it through another pulley fixed in the floor of the stage. The on-stage top corner of one curtain is attached to one part of the line, and that of the other to the return part. Then when (*b*) is pulled the curtains open and when (*a*) is pulled, they close. It is useful to put a distinguishing mark on

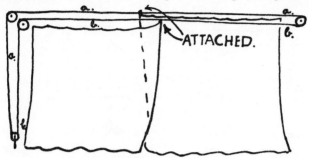

Fig. *129. Separate detail of working lines. This diagram emphasizes the fact that the curtains are only attached to the working lines at one point each. The suspension of the curtains by the rings is from the two strained wires in Fig. 128, which are omitted from this figure.*

(*a*) such as a few turns of insulating tape, to avoid pulling the wrong line.

The outer ring of either curtain should be tied in position to some fixed point such as the wire strainer, to prevent its sliding inwards and showing a gap between curtain and proscenium. On big stages the whole outer side of each curtain

Fig. *130. A similar arrangement to Fig. 128 but with separate battens for each half of the curtain: the pair overlapped and bolted in the centre.*

may be anchored at intervals to the proscenium so as to keep in place.

On occasion it may be more convenient to use, above the curtains, two short separate battens instead of one long one, and, overlapping them at the centre, bolt them together at two points about a foot apart as in Fig. 130.

Some dozen other methods of working the front curtains may be added. Fig. 131 shows an old-fashioned 'drop' (back view), where the top edge of the cloth is fastened to a fixed batten that carries a pulley screwed to its face at either end. At the bottom of the cloth is fixed a roller (probably hollow,

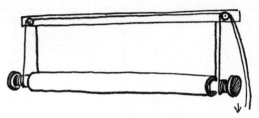

Fig. 131. The working of the roller drop.

and made of 1 in. wide laths nailed to circular core-pieces), and at the end of the roller it is convenient to have a larger disc to prevent the rope riding off. This rope is led through the pulleys (one of which is a double pulley) and each end is attached to one end of the roller when the cloth is hanging in place but *rolled up*. Now when the lines are not held, the weight of the roller unrolls the cloth and simultaneously *rolls up* the lines around that falling-roller. A pull on the two lines twists the roller and turns it up, winding the cloth as it goes, and at its limit the lines are secured to a cleat. The important point is to see that the lines wind round the roller in the opposite direction to the cloth.

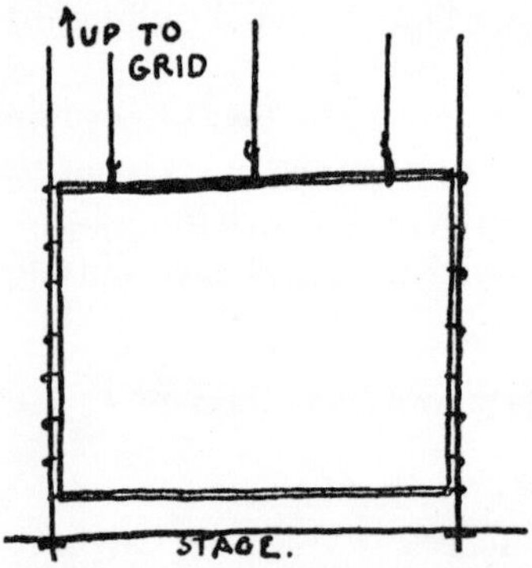

Fig. 132. The simple drop working between guide-wires.

Fig. 132 shows the 'drop' in a theatre which possesses 'flying-space' above the stage, so that the cloth can simply be pulled up out of sight without rolling. Notice the guide-wires strained at either side of the curtain, around which reach special rings at intervals, fixed to the curtain itself, so that it shall descend directly into place and not be blown backwards or forwards.

Fig. 133 shows a simple tube bent to shape so as to serve as the railway for both curtains and allow overlap in the centre.

Fig. 134 shows a separate strained wire used for each cur-

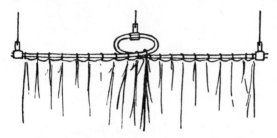

Fig. 133. A curved tube used as a curtain rail.

tain, anchored to the wall at either end. The curtain line (not shown) is endless and works through two pulleys attached to the walls.

One of the chief objections to our ordinary curtain railway is noise. And anyone who has had an opportunity of comparing a soft silent closing like an owl's wing with the pigeon's

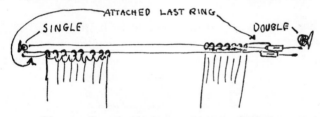

Fig. 134. Curtains running on separate strained wires.

roar of the ordinary runners, knows the greater dramatic effect of silence. It is to gain something of this effect that the fibre bobbin is used (Fig. 135), for all the world like a cotton-reel with a webbing tag to it; it is threaded on a strained wire like a ring is, or on a less tight wire (which then serves only to retain it in place), when it rests its weight on two parallel rods of metal on the principle diagrammatically shown in

Fig. 136. Two of these arrangements are bolted together with ends overlapping like the battens in Fig. 130 and so form the system of some of the best commercial curtain railways.

Fig. 135. A curtain bobbin.

Fig. 136. Sectional detail of bobbin and track.

Fig. 137 shows a variant in which, instead of a simple ring, a fibre ball with a wire attachment runs in what approximates to a horizontal tube with a slit along the lower side

Fig. 137. Alternative ball form of bobbin.

Fig. 138. Detail of simple home-made track for Fig. 137.

Such a conduit can be home-made by bolting together one length of 1 in. × 1 in. batten and two lengths of 2 in. × 1 in. (Fig. 138). Retaining-strips, either of metal or hardwood, are

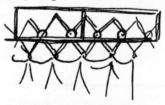

Fig. 139. Elaborate apparatus for bunching tabs evenly as they are closed.

then screwed to the undersides of the 2 in. × 1 in. battens with enough gap between to allow play to the wire attachment on the ball, into which the curtain is hooked. The track in which the set of balls slides may be greased to facilitate the running, or lubricated with domestic 'black lead' mixed to a thick creamy consistency with water and applied with a brush.

Fig. 139 shows an elaborate trellis railway designed simply to prevent unequal bunching as the curtains withdraw.

Fig. 140 represents several points in the working of the decorative but more bulky 'drapes'. Drawn in ordinary lines is the simplest form with indications of the series of points at which the diagonal, curving line is led through rings attached to the back of the curtain, and also the more or less heavy

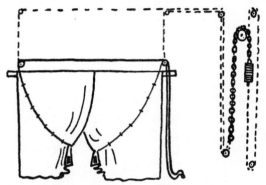

Fig. 140. Details of the working of 'Drapes'.

weight that is fixed to the inner lower corner of each curtain to pull it down. (One of these weights, incidentally, can give a quite sufficiently unpleasant blow if it catches you on the elbow joint in descending—even on a small stage. On a large stage the blow may be serious.) The rest of the diagram in dotted lines shows the continuation of the system on a larger stage, and this point is to be noticed—as the linesman begins to open his curtains, he need exert very little strength—even a twitch would open them almost as far as the diagram shows —but as the opening increases, more and more of the weight of the bunch is caught up and the final stages need consider-able power. It is for this reason that the ingenious special counterweight system is used as shown in the figure. Note that from the counterweight, upwards and over its special pulley, a section of the line is of especial thickness. This represents a section of heavy chain whose links one by one add increasing weight to the counterweight as they come over the

Fig. 141. A conical winch-drum for overcoming increasing weight.

pulley towards it, and so progressively assist to counter-balance the increasing weight of the opening curtain.

Lastly, in Fig. 141, is shown a winch with a conical drum, again intended to assist, by a greater leverage at the end, the overcoming of the growing weight of the opening drapes.

CHAPTER THREE

Pure Curtain Settings for the Proscenium Stage

SECTION 11

The Curtains

Now we can draw breath for a moment before facing a new situation in our development of setting, and we can survey the position.

We are no longer faced with a bare platform in our simple hall. We have, instead, a proscenium, a solid framework across the hall, with an opening in the middle behind which the stage has receded. We have now to consider not only the design of a background to the acting-area, with side extensions possible though not essential, but a design for three dimensions, those of the back, the sides and the top, where all these are essential.

Furthermore, on the technical side, we have this benefit to take into account, that for the first time it is possible to hang our scenery from above, without supporting ropes and gear being visible from the auditorium.

We are, in short, on the verge of the full theatre set. Before, however, we can reckon ourselves to be completely ready to use fuller methods of setting with all their particularities there is one further factor to be brought in—the height of the roof or ceiling above the stage and behind the proscenium. If the stage ceiling is only a few feet above the top of the proscenium opening, then our handling of scenery will be very different from what it would be if the ceiling were more than twice the height of that opening, when we should be able to call the high loft above the stage the 'flies', and draw our scenery out of sight up into it as a means of scene-change.

Between the two alternatives of full flying space and a low ceiling near to the proscenium, there are intermediate altitudes where special modifications of scene-handling can be used. Before we devise a curtain set for a fully-equipped stage, let us examine in detail one designed to go on the stage with no flying room, and so follow the steady line of development of our simple settings. The making of the Full Curtain Set for a proscenium-stage we will discuss from the point at which we may suppose a designer entering with no materials and everything to make from the beginning.

Given a stage and a proscenium, for putting up a curtain set, he will first decide the material and colour of the curtains, in order to send in his specification. For material I suggest, as likely to meet average requirements, a wool or wool-mixture fabric, Bolton Sheeting, or Government Silk if that is still to be obtained. All these materials hang fairly well, do not easily crease, and they do not easily allow any lights there may be in the wings to be seen through them.

A good set of velvets of course is the best. It has a very long life and an excellent appearance. But if velvet proves too expensive the next choice may be Bolton Sheeting or a material of that sort. You can buy Bolton Sheeting in several colours and if it does not, as a material, 'take the light' as well as velvet, it has at any rate a certain character and texture in its folds.

Government Silk, which I believe is a difficult material now to get, is thinner than Bolton Sheeting and hangs with a leaner fold, but it will serve very well as a next best.

A wool fabric has many advantages—it hangs well, is fairly thick and you can choose your colours, but its greatest importance is that it is naturally flame-proof. It will not burst into flame when set alight, it merely blackens, crumbles and smoulders, and so it is that, in any hall of public entertainment where the Government's rules apply or which is under a local council's jurisdiction, 'any permanent hangings and curtains which may be permitted by the council shall be of heavy woollen material only. . . . And temporary decorations shall not be used except with the consent of the council in writing. Application . . . must be accompanied by samples of the material. . . .'

I am quoting from the *Rules with regard to the Management of Places of Public Entertainment*, published by the London County Council. It is a pamphlet costing 6d., and is of great importance to anyone concerned with the staging of a show for public performance; we shall return to it later. Concerning the material for curtains, Miss May Padman of Yorkshire has written me the following note:

'Cognate considerations which are too frequently ignored in the choice of curtain materials are the weave, or surface, of the cloth and the amount of light available in any given theatre. Materials which, under ordinary artificial light, seem to be the same shade of silver grey, for example, will re-act very differently under stage conditions. This is partly because the directed beams from the lighting set will strike the surface at less widely diverse angles, and partly because the threads are differently arranged according to the fabric.

'In woven materials there are minute pits, where each thread crosses its neighbour, and each of these is a tiny trap to catch and retain light. A close-cut velvet is to light as blotting-paper is to ink because the reflecting area of the ends of its fibres is less than the absorbing area of the spaces between. Chenille curtain velvet, reflecting from the sides of its threads, gives back more light but only so long as its surface remains unruffled. Woollen material, with its slightly fluffy face, and bolton sheeting, woven in herring-bone or in diagonal pattern, reflects comparatively little light. Hessian with its slightly-glazed, flat threads woven under and over, 'one and one', has a comparatively high power of reflection but it must be lined unless the spill from backstage floods is to reveal figures waiting in the wings. The shiny threads of artificial silk will absorb very little light, particularly if we choose what is known as a 'warp' cloth where the long threads lie close together on the surface. Such a material has a metallic lustre for its high lights and an extraordinary depth of tone in its shadows. Casement cloth and other cotton fabrics are inexpensive and do not absorb too much light, but they lack the weight which gives such richness to velvet and to woollen curtains.

'Some of these materials are more easily stored than others. When they have to be packed curtains should be rolled evenly from the bottom so that any unavoidable creases occur near the top where the weight of the folds will the more quickly straighten them next time they are used. Of all the fabrics wool resists creases best, then velvet. Hessian does not lose its freshness so easily as cotton goods whilst the otherwise-desirable artificial silks crease very easily and are difficult to smooth. Government silk, if obtainable, is excellent and, if backstage lights are very carefully masked, it may be used without lining.

'Why have we stressed so heavily the effect of light on texture? Because we are convinced that some stages are wrongly supposed to be badly lighted. It is possible to have a reasonably good lighting set and yet fail to secure the desired effects simply because the curtains have been chosen only for colour and draping. Select the material which will give back the maximum degree of light which your equipment can produce. If there is more than you need for some plays, cut down the light but do not condemn your producer to work in twilight unless he wishes to do so.'

For the colour of the curtains, there is a very pertinent question to ask at the outset, 'What sort of grey should one have?'

If you will understand me to use the word 'grey' in the widest sense, the question makes a very practical approach.

The decision to be made is: In your particular case is the grey to err on the warm, light side to fawns or even dull yellows, or on the warm, dark side to browns, or is it to err on the cold side to variations of steels, of light and dark blues?

It is easier to begin with a grey in your mind and discuss and decide on a modification in one direction or another of the nature of the grey, than to begin with the choice of many hues which are embarrassing in their profusion and, once mentioned, tend to be chosen for their names' sake rather than for their colour-suitability to the type of show most often to be played before them. Take into account the effect of dark colours on comedy, and the effect on light colours of much handling and of dirt.

Think, then, first of a grey, then of the type or types of

show you would give, and you will find it quite amusing to decide in what direction the nature of those types of show pushes your choice of a grey.

If you are ordering your material from a firm which specializes in theatrical stuffs, such as B. Burnet's of 22 Garrick Street, Long Acre, London, W.C. 2, you can specify that it be fireproofed before it is delivered to you. The fireproofing of a large amount of material is not an easy job for the amateur, but the *Rules for the Regulation of Places of Public Entertainment*, mentioned a little while ago, gives two recipes for making a fireproofing solution.

I would add the warning that if you fireproof a material yourself with any solution, home-made or bought, you should impregnate and dry only a sample of that material first, because upon certain substances certain solutions have a deleterious effect. If all is well you can go ahead; if the sample is spoiled, you must experiment with some of the other solutions before you tackle the whole quantity.

One of the most complete treatises on fireproofing materials is issued by His Majesty's Stationery Office for the Department of Scientific and Industrial Research and is *The Second Report of the Fabrics Co-ordinating Committee*, 1930. It costs five shillings.

As to the curtains themselves, it is of the first importance to see that the material is bought in strips and *kept in strips*, not sewn together into large areas sufficient to cover the complete back or side of the stage.

By far the most useful and practical arrangement of curtain set is one where the 'walls' of curtain are composed of three-foot strips hanging side by side, any of which may be detached or part-rolled to make an opening or accommodate a piece of scenery at any part of the stage at need. To seam these strips into one huge curtain is to reduce their possibilities ten-fold.

The curtains should not only be in strips, but in strips of a standard width; then we shall be able to set, let us say, a single door in the space of any one curtain-strip, a double door or French window in the space of two, a triple-arch or set of long steps in the space of three . . . and so forth.

THE CURTAINS

We have now to consider, first the most flexible method of hanging such a set of curtains, that is to say the method that will most readily allow us to make scenes of any desired depth or shape compatible with our stage: secondly, the standardizing and making of the curtain strips themselves: lastly, their use and the setting among them of details of scenery.

SECTION 12

The Battens and Lines for Hanging

The means of hanging may be roughly described as a large square horizontal frame slung from pulleys, with the curtains tied round three sides. For this it is essential that we should have at least four pulleys in the roof above the stage. If our theatre were fully equipped with flies, we should simply choose two of the many sets of lines, taking those in the most convenient position. If our theatre has a proscenium of the second type I described, from whose top two overhead beams run across the stage to the back wall, we should select the most suitable positions and screw four pulley-blocks into the beams.

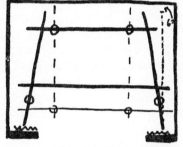

Fig. 142. Plan of the frame of battens for hanging a curtain set.

Or if our theatre has a plain ceiling in which four pulleys are already fixed and no other fixture is permitted we should note carefully the position of those blocks and arrange our curtain set so that it could be hung from these points: that might involve certain modifications in the arrangement I am going to describe, as we shall see.

The system of *fit-up* which we shall hang from the pulleys—the frame to which the curtains will be fixed—is very simple. We need four battens; a back batten, two side battens and a border batten. The first three will hang directly over the limits of our acting-area, and the fourth in whatever place we decide is best for the border (Fig. 142, thick lines).

Each batten should be of 3 in. × 2 in. wood. The back batten should be four feet longer than the back line of the acting-
area, to project two feet at either end. The side battens should
reach from the 'tabs' (the front curtain)—just so far away
from them as to ensure their free working—to overlap the
back batten by two feet if there is room, but special care
should be taken, if the back wall of the stage is plastered for
use as a sky, that the side battens be at least a good six inches
shorter than the direct distance from the tabs to the plaster
back wall, otherwise the risk of scratches on the plaster is
heavy, and a scratched sky must be avoided at all costs. Finally, the border batten should be two feet longer than the
width of the acting-area at the level of the border.

That is the disposition and dimension of the battens; now
what about their means of suspension? If we lay the back batten upon the stage in its approximate position, next lay the
side-battens in their places, resting their up-stage ends upon
the back batten, and lastly lay the border batten across the
sides, we can suspend the whole frame from four pulleys
placed as indicated by the circles on the heavy lines in Fig.
142 and if you have yet to fix your pulleys, you will be able to
place them as in the diagram. But if they are already there it
is probable that the sets are in two parallel lines, from back
to front—the dotted lines in the diagram. You will then have
to hang your border beneath one of these sets of lines and if
this necessitates altering its position noticeably, it may entail
altering its depth to mask. But there ought to be enough
pulleys for you to choose a pair that will hang your border
pretty near where you have planned it. You will, however,
have to suspend your border batten and rest the sides upon
it. The border batten would then be beneath.

Or if you can find no position of pulleys at which to suspend
the border, then you must use a fifth batten somewhere about
the level of the thin line in the diagram and rest your sides on
the ends of this fifth batten, and rest your border batten, at
whatever point you choose, upon the sides.

The next thing is to see where the lines or down-ropes
from the pulleys tie off, that is, where and to what the ends of
the ropes by which the load is hauled up are made fast. And

if the pulleys are still to be fixed, observe which side of the stage will offer the freest space for the descending ends and their cleats.

We may, on a very small stage with a very light curtain set, take the line from each pulley individually as it descends and make it fast to the most convenient point—even to a large screw-eye or a stage-screw fixed into the stage beneath that pulley (Fig. 143).

Fig. 143. The suspension of the frame. (1) The simplest direct tie-off.

For larger stages and heavier curtains it is much more workmanlike to gather the two lines from each pair of pulleys and make them off together (Fig. 144). You work them simultaneously and your battens can be pulled up level.

In most cases all the lines should tie off on the same side of the stage, but the structural conditions of the stage walls may make it necessary to tie off the down-stage sets of lines on one side and the up-stage lines on the other.

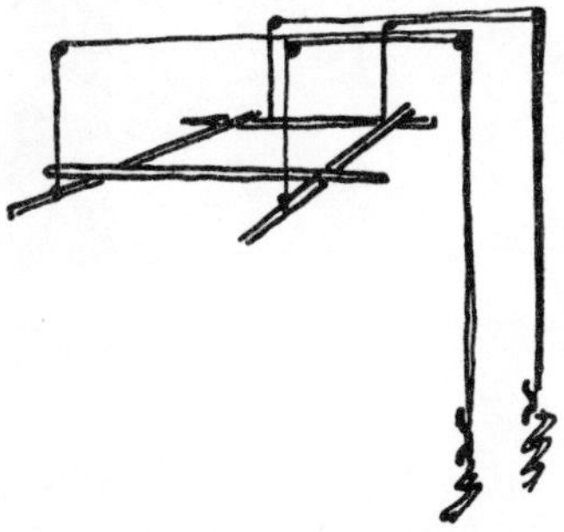

In any case each pair of pulleys will be supplied with a *long* and a *short* line. And you may find on larger stages where longer battens—say between twenty and thirty feet—are used that a *centre* line is also needed (Fig. 145).

If then we decide to tie off our lines in pairs (or in threes if our battens are very long and would sag without a centre line; for the sake of brevity I shall assume here we need only two lines), we must fix a single-sheave block (that is a pulley-block with one wheel) for the long line and a single-sheave for the short line, and a double-sheave block as a head block to gather the two lines together and return them down to the

Fig. 144. (2) A better method of tie-off using side pulleys or 'head blocks'.

stage. If we omit the head block and tie off these lines directly from the short-line-block, which will then have to be double, you will realize by Fig. 146 how the descending lines obstruct

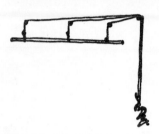

Fig. 145. (3) A typical arrangement of lines.

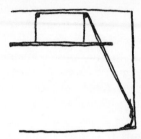

Fig. 146. (4) The obstruction
of the wings caused by omitting
the head blocks at the side.

the wings and may hinder movement and the shifting of furniture and properties.

The normal attachment of line to batten is by the knot shown in Fig. 147, but it may happen that, in certain cir-

Fig. 147. (5) Stages in the knot used to attach the battens to the hanging lines. The stage hand is to be imagined standing with his back to you and to the right side of the line, his left hand would hold the batten and his right would cross his body in front to tie the knot. In the last stage the batten is already suspended and both his hands are free to finish the end.

cumstances, it is impractical to put more than two pulleys in the roof for each batten but that these battens are long enough, owing to the large size of the stage, to sag or at any rate to present a risk if not suspended at a third point. Then a bridle should be used (Fig. 148). It is with chain bridles that the heavy lamp battens are often hung from wire cables. In some cases, with heavy curtains and when the down-stage pulleys are not over the side battens and the set is carried on the border batten or the fifth batten, you may need a centre line or bridles for that border or fifth batten.

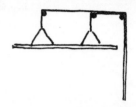

If you are tolerably certain that the same shape of acting-area will always be used on your stage, you may drill the battens at the four points where they cross and pin them with a nut and bolt. The battens can then be labelled and taken apart to store when not in use. But if, as I think will be more likely, you

Fig. 148. (6) Showing the use of bridles to offer twice the points of support to a long batten, that would sag with less.

prefer the idea of keeping your acting-area elastic, you may, and this is the beauty of this method, lash the crossings of your battens with rope, and space them, each time you use them, to suit your current needs.

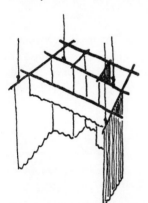

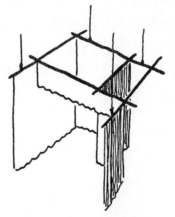

Fig. 149. Arrangements of the frame. (1) For a bay in the back wall.

Fig. 150. (2) For a break-forward in a side wall.

The desirability of a flexible fit-up frame is worth stressing, and the method described is capable of more variations than any other. Some of the widely diverse arrangements of frame battens will be seen in Figs. 149 to 152. In all these examples the set is hung from four pulleys. Fig. 149 shows a square bay in the back wall. Fig. 150 shows a break forward in the side wall. Fig. 151 shows a set with a diagonal back for which the border will need to be shortened. Fig. 152 shows how, by a determined designer, the curtains may even be hung in a

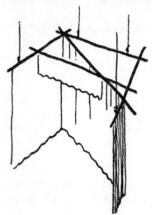
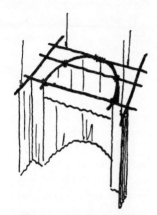

Fig. 151. (3) For a diagonal back wall.

Fig. 152. (4) For a curved wall.

curve, from a bent metal tube, or even, in small light sets, a row of stout canes tightly bound end to end, lashed upon the cross-battens of the frame. In short, it is possible by this method to hang a curtain set approximately to any plan one may be given, by arrangement and supplementing of the battens.

Fig. 153. Plan of a side batten with diagonal grooves for alternative wing-setting of side curtains.

A further refinement may be made in the provision of means for hanging the side strips either in a continuous wall as shown above, or each at an angle, making a row of wings. Fig. 153 shows a plan, looking up, of a side batten in which a number of diagonal halve-grooves has been cut to correspond with the centre-top of each curtain strip. The strips are nailed each to a separate short batten and every one of these is bolted

at the centre through the middle of its groove. The screw end
of the bolt projects upwards (Fig. 153a), and before the nut is
applied a coiled spring and a washer is put on and the nut

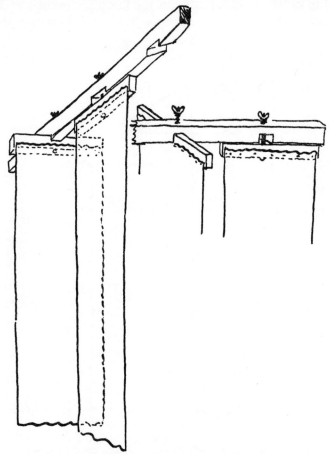

*Fig. 153a. The arrangement of grooves with spring-bolts for
alternative plain or wing setting of the side curtains.*

tightened on that when the batten is in the position shown on
the right of the figure. If now the fit-up is in place and a stage
hand takes hold of each edge of the curtain below, and pulls
it gently, the batten and curtain will come slightly away and
may be twisted until the batten is parallel with the groove

127

and, under the pressure of the spring, slips up into it and remains at that angle till pulled downwards and twisted again. Such a method ensures the wings remaining at the set angle but in practice somewhat limits the flexibility of the set. (It means, for instance, that all cross battens must be laid over the

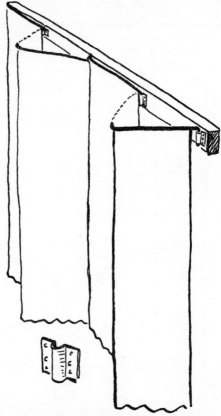

Fig. 153b. Another method using pivoted side-arms for the wings.

side battens, and the hanging-lines attached only to the side battens, and by screw-eyes.) An alternative method to be preferred in some circumstances is therefore suggested in Fig. 153*b*. Here the side batten is provided with metal sockets at intervals corresponding with the joins of the curtain strips. Into the sockets metal rods with turned ends are dropped and the curtains fixed to these pivoted arms, when any strip can be swung to any angle. The arms should slope very slightly up from the pivot so that the curtains may overlap a little when flat. With this method the arms may be taken off when not needed and the battens can be arranged to plans almost as varied as before. A little special care, however, is needed in both these methods in the placing of the border or borders.

A further point sometimes of considerable value is the 'top-joining' of the back curtains, and their suspension upon traverse wires so that they may either be used as a plain back wall as usual, with any curtain strip, or strips, part-rolled for such details of doors and so forth as may be necessary, or the whole may be opened in the centre and drawn aside like the tabs to give a central opening varying in width according to the amount the curtains are drawn.

Such an arrangement entails a little complication. Perhaps the most practical method of adapting is this:

Keep in store an additional back batten—a stoutish one, possibly 4 in. × 2½ in.—furnished exactly as was the bearer of the tabs shown in Fig. 128, save that the inner end of either wire should not be fixed directly to its staple but should end in a strong snap-hook so that it can be disengaged from the staple at will in order to slip on the curtain-rings, which are here not permanently threaded on the wire but sewn to the curtain bands, as we shall see in a moment.

For a normal curtain set the plain back batten is used, but when a 'traverse-back' is needed, the special heavier batten will take its place. Upon this the same curtains are fixed in a special way which we will outline as soon as we have described the method for the normal set without a traverse-back.

Having noticed the value of this traverse curtain, of whose use we shall have a special instance later in Section 24 when we discuss the staging of an Elizabethan play, we shall soon find that it is available not only for use instead of the simple back curtains, but also as an addition to them and running lower down stage—say at half depth, or near the front to close off a shallow fore-stage for apron scenes, while a full-stage scene is being prepared behind. On such occasions, the simple frame may be assembled in the usual way with the plain back batten, and the traverse batten may then be lashed across in addition *under* the side battens at whatever stage depth you please. You will then, of course, need an extra set of curtains to form that traverse wall.

When the battens are assembled we pull on our lines and lift the whole framework to about elbow height ready to tie on the curtains. Let us return to these curtains.

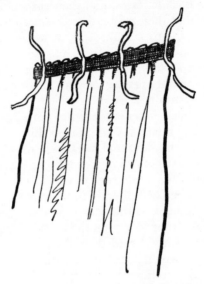

Fig. 154. A curtain strip on its web with its tying-tapes.

The curtain material, we will suppose, has arrived and is cut up and ready to gather. If we have chosen to use curtains, say, 14 ft. high, we cut our roll into lengths of 14 ft. 4 in. (the inches for turnings) and gather each piece to its decided width on a band of 2 in. webbing (such as upholsterers use to cross under the bottoms of chairs) and as long as the folded curtain is wide.

Generally we may take it that a minimum of fullness is given by allowing a third or half as much stuff again to a given space, but it is a question for yourself to decide whether the extra fullness of appearance that half-as-much-again gives will compensate for a slight extra difficulty in handling and rolling if the curtains are to be used with doors and windows in the way I shall describe; generally, as the most convenient width of curtain material is 50 in., that is 4 ft. 2 in., we may count each width when gathered into fullness as three feet, which is a very good standard width.

The webbing band is at the upper end of each curtain and to it will be sewn, at intervals of about 9 in., strips of strong tape each about 18 in. long (Fig. 154). These are to tie the curtains to the battens. The curtains will need hemming top and bottom, but if you have used the full width of the

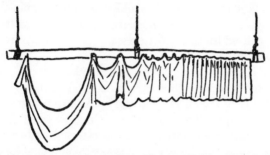

Fig. 155. Attaching the border. If the border is attached direct to the batten, to preserve equal folds the two ends and the centre are attached first, then the points midway between these and so on.

stuff there will already be a selvedge up either side. You may insert chains in the lower hem if necessary.

It is a good plan to cut two curtains up the middle so as to give four, narrow, half-width curtains, and the raw edge must be hemmed. The use of these narrow curtains will be explained. The border (or borders) is then cut to size, hemmed, gathered and provided with tying tapes, or is nailed directly to the batten (Fig. 155).

You have now in theory merely to tie your curtains side by side to their battens by their tapes, working round till you have enclosed the whole acting-area, fit your border, haul on your lines to lift the battens to the length of the curtains and you have a curtain set.

But before you can call your set of curtains a setting for a show, there are several modifications and an almost

131

innumerable range of permutations to help you to make them no dumb background but an eloquent part of the play and a valuable factor in the show.

First of all you will discover that, if your curtains hang edge to edge, they will easily part and allow gaps through which the space in the wings can be seen. So you overlap each curtain on its neighbour,[1] taking care that, on the sides, each curtain overlaps its *up-stage* neighbour while its down-stage edge lies *behind* the edge of the neighbour on that side. Otherwise you will still have gaps in your curtains.

The overlap need not be more than a couple of inches but those inches mount up and make an appreciable factor in your original estimate for material. They may easily make a further full-width curtain necessary above the number you have calculated.

There is only one exception to the rule of overlapping up-stage neighbour, and that exception gives us the guide to the overlapping of the curtains at the back, and it takes us to the complicated question of openings, which we must discuss be - fore we consider the principle of overlap any further.

As we shall have, however, to make a somewhat long development before we have sufficient data to formulate this rule of overlap, we may add a note here on the special hanging of the back curtains when it is proposed to use them as a traverse that can be opened and closed; we shall then be able to keep our treatment of the fit-up and its arrangement complete in one place and put off only this question of overlaps and openings to be settled after further study.

The curtains to be hung at the back are here not to be tied by tapes to the battens, but suspended by rings from a wire. There should be eight of these rings to each 3-ft. curtain-width. They must be strong enough to bear the weight of the

---

[1] Instead of overlapping, some stage-managers join the edges of each pair of adjacent curtains by means of a couple of spring clothes-pegs. Those large bulldog spring clips that are used for holding batches of papers together have a longer gripping surface than clothes-pegs. They are useful even when the curtains are already overlapped. One clip is about five feet from the ground at each join and another at the level of the actors' hands. With crinolines or swords you may need two more below the lower clip. It is cheapest to buy them by the gross.

curtain without being pulled out of their circular shape. Each of the curtains normally used in the back (and one further one which is now needed to compensate for the extra overlap in the centre) should be furnished with these rings sewn upon their webbing band in addition to the tapes. They do not hinder the ordinary tying of curtain to batten when the curtain is hung in the normal way.

When the back curtains are needed to form a traverse, the frame of battens is assembled on the stage and lashed in the usual way save that the stouter batten, provided with wires as in Fig. 128, replaces the plain one at the back. The fit-up is

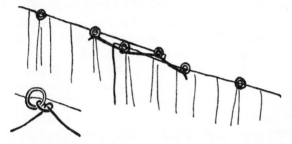

Fig. 156. Method of retaining the even overlap of top-joined curtain strips used as a traverse, so that they may be pulled either way without parting. Below, detail of knot.

then pulled up to shoulder height as before and the side curtains tied on by their tapes. At the back, however, the wires are unhooked at the centre and the curtain strips now threaded on the wire by their rings, the tapes hanging loose behind. Overlap is attained in this way: The stage-right curtain of the back wall is threaded on all except its last ring; before that is put on the wire, the first ring of the next curtain is slipped on, then the last ring of the original curtain comes after that, followed by the remaining rings of the second curtain, until again its last ring is reached, when that is similarly preceded by the first ring of the third curtain and so on. When both wires have received their complement of curtain-strips, the snap-hooks are clipped on their staples and the wire-strainers tightened. The strips are then regularized and in order to preserve the regular overlap the following precaution is taken at the back of each join; a string is threaded through the four rings nearest to the overlap, tying them together so that they are prevented from sliding apart farther than ensures an adequate overlap (Fig. 156), and, this done, you have only to thread your working-line on as in Fig. 129 and your traverse-back-wall is ready and your set may be pulled up to its full height.

Once it is hung you will probably find that a vigorous use of the traverse curtain-lines tends to make the set sway, then a large screw-eye should be inserted into the top of the back batten at either end, and this tethered to the side wall of the stage or another convenient fixed point by means of a line. It is desirable, if you are hanging your set from the minimum four pulleys, to suspend this heavier back batten by bridles as in Fig. 148. This limitation in which only four attachments may be made in the structure of the building does not fortunately apply to every stage. For those stages where screw-eyes or eye-bolts may be fixed in wall or ceiling at will, there is another simpler method of hanging a traverse in which the strained wires are independent of the fit-up frame and are attached to the side walls as Fig. 134 shows.

Further, if the traverse curtains are very light, we may make an even simpler arrangement where only one wire is used for the pair of curtains. This is the method used, for instance, by Mr. Sladen-Smith in the theatre of the Unnamed Society, Manchester. There the realistic type of play with a straight interior setting is rarely chosen. Instead, painted and decorative sets are most frequently used together with a number of specially designed front curtains.

The method used involves one wire only, makes a feature of a centre support for that wire and still manages to overlap the closed curtains in the centre. In Fig. 157 a wire is strained between the two side walls with its centre supported by a cord from the roof above. The feature of this cord is not primarily its support, but the means it offers of adjusting within small limits the hang of the closed curtains (at least at the centre where it most matters), so that by tightening and loosening the cord they may be made to hang just to touch the stage. Overlap in the centre is achieved by attaching the top corner of the front curtain *not to a ring* but only to the working-line, as in Fig. 157. Then, provided the lines are kept taut when the curtains are drawn, an overlap equal to the distance from corner to first ring will be maintained. In order to keep the lines taut, a ring may be threaded on the bottom of the loop of the line where it approaches the floor, and this tethered to

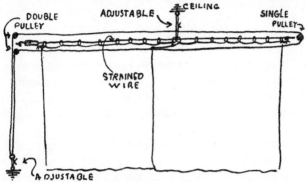

Fig 157. Mechanism of a light traverse with centre overlap but running on a single wire.

a screw-eye in the floor by means of a string. Such a temporary fixing is an advantage because it can be undone after each performance and adjusted before the next so that, whatever weather and heat conditions, the tautness of the lines may be kept constant. The working-lines and pulleys for a light traverse may sometimes be reduced to no more than stout cord and screw-eyes.

We may now begin to consider the question of openings and eventually we shall see how they affect the overlap of the curtains.

SECTION 13

Openings and Backings

How are the actors to enter and leave the acting-area that your curtains surround? Are they to push the curtains aside as they choose or will you give them specific openings? If you use wing-sides the problem solves itself. Otherwise, what is to be done?

An actor is often very partial to an appearance through curtains, but the stage manager is not, for though the actor may make a good entrance for himself he never can grow to see that he should leave the curtains hanging beautifully—and the stage manager looks up from his prompt book (if he has no A.S.M.) and sees the gap in the curtains and angrily hurries round to set them right. It needs an almost impossible amount of drilling to make an ordinary actor see that he does not disarrange the curtains.

The difficulties are so great that we will consider at once providing him with entrances that relieve him of all necessity for touching the curtains. He will then disarrange them only about half as much as before.

It is a very vexed question in the theatre whether actual practicable doors and windows should or should not be used with a curtain set. The Purists say, 'Certainly not. Curtains are curtains, it is foolish to pretend they are walls, and to have a door you must have a wall. The only natural entrance in curtains is to part the curtains and fix them back, or roll them up, or shorten them to leave an opening. To put a wooden sash- or casement-window among your curtains is an anomaly.'

To a certain extent I agree with this. If you 'play in curtains' then call your curtains curtains and let there be nothing but your ingenuity and arrangement to convert them into a setting. But only with this proviso: That you limit your choice of plays strictly to such as lend themselves to production in a pure curtain set. That cuts out a large number of modern-dress, more or less realistic dramas and comedies. You may

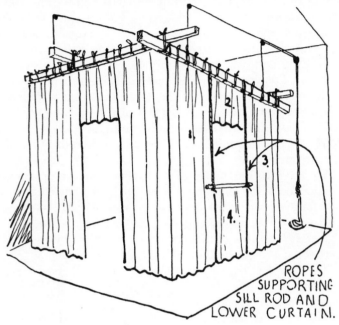

ROPES
SUPPORTING
SILL ROD AND
LOWER CURTAIN.

Fig. 158. Openings in the curtains.

play *Count Albany* or *Hippolytus* in pure curtains if you will, but you can't do *The Thirteenth Chair*, or *The Middle Watch*. However, my function is not to decide the controversy for you but to indicate methods of procedure for either course.

One method of the pure-curtain school is to make the openings by using a short curtain (Fig. 158) specially made to hang about seven feet off the ground and capable of being tied to the batten in the same way as the long curtains, in a gap in the run specially left for it.

For the windows, a curtain similar to the over-door curtain (2 in Fig. 158) is tied to the batten above, and at either

137

side a length of cord hangs down. The two cords reach to the bottom of what is to be the window opening, where they suspend a wooden rod; on this rod is hung a piece of curtain to fill in between the 'window-sill' and the ground (Fig. 158, 4).

But for the purist in curtains, I think a better way to make the opening is to omit a curtain altogether in the run where the entrance is needed. This gives a tall dignified door perfectly in keeping with the long folds of the curtains and with the 'curtain' atmosphere—which is always rather romantic and grand-hall-like.

I have known windows achieved in such pure curtain sets in exactly the same way as the doors, save that a table was placed to stand across the bottom of the opening, covered with a long cloth that fell to the ground all round. Alternatively the opening might be blocked by a chest or other such piece of furniture.

We have to remember that element which is frequently overlooked in the planning of a set, the backing to each opening, for every opening—door, window or fireplace—in whatever part of the stage, must be provided with a backing, so that the view through that opening is never of unwanted corners of the 'wings' or of actors waiting for their cues.

The simplest backing for a door is a two-leaved screen, high enough to mask from the front row of the stalls when the door is open (Fig. 159).

The simplest backing for a window is a plain, pale-blue sky-sheet—a piece of canvas, sized and painted, or dyed—with any additional piece of scenery set in front of it, such as a profile tree, or an actual bough, or a street lamp to mark the locality and give character to the outlook. This exterior backing will need to be well-lit with a standard flood-lamp placed on the stage beside it.

One advantage of a plastered back wall to the stage is that windows in the back curtains of a set never need any other special backing. The aspect is always there. In default of a plastered back wall, a sky-cloth may be hung from a batten, suspended from the ends of the side-battens of the fit-up frame, that we left projecting behind the back curtains of our set (Fig. 159). And it must be hung free from folds.

But the curtain purist may protest that the backing to an opening in a pure curtain set should also consist of hung curtains in folds. Then he may either hang a curtain over the double screen we have mentioned and stand that behind his door. Or he may make use of the projecting ends of either the border-batten, or the back-batten, from which to hang his backing curtains (Fig. 160). He will need to be careful to see

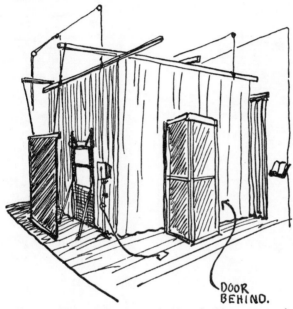

DOOR
BEHIND.

Fig. 159. *Back view of set showing backings to openings.* (*The lead to the standard flood-lamp is knotted round the stand before being plugged into the lamp so that a clumsy foot will be less likely to disconnect the lamp.*)

that he masks on his cross sight-lines and he will perhaps be forced to use longer battens to give a greater projection from which to hang his backing than if he used screens.

He may even decide that the sky outside his windows must consist of curtains hung in folds like his set-wall curtains. And because he accepts such a definite convention so frankly, he may obtain some very successful results by pouring contrasting lighting on the curtains that represent the exterior through his window, and the curtains that make his set walls. Admirable effects are sometimes made by lighting the exterior curtains dimly and from the side, or from below, for night scenes.

When Miss Lena Ashwell's Players used to tour the suburbs, the very wide range of plays presented demanded that doors

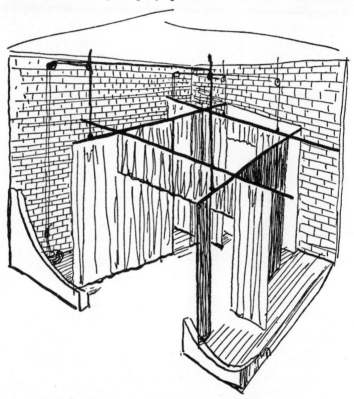

Fig. 160. Backings hung on extensions of the frame battens.

and windows should be more realistically represented, and in the course of the company's development the stage staff evolved a technique which may be our introduction to the other less 'pure' school of curtain users.

The system of the Lena Ashwell Players was to hang a curtain fit-up of exactly the sort we have described for the pure curtain setting, as a kind of permanent neutral basis for every scene they staged: then against, or in, that background they set certain *details* of scenery, either practicable doors, etc., or painted set-pieces, by the change and rearrangement of which they effected the transition from scene to scene in every play.

I shall leave the further discussion of this technique till the next chapter on Detail Setting, to which it more properly belongs, and confine myself here to the Pure Curtain Setting, of which we will now go on to describe two other useful examples.

SECTION 14

The 'Armed-Batten' Curtain Set and the 'Rochdale Curtain Theatre' Set

Of the last two forms of curtain setting I have to describe, the first is that used in full theatres where a quick and complete striking of the set may be necessary, and the system of curtain-hanging must be capable of being 'flown away', or

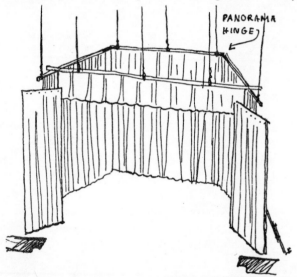

PANORAMA HINGE

Fig. 161. The armed-batten arrangement for a curtain set.

lifted clear up into the flies, without occupying undue space up there.

The examination of the grid and the counterweight system and all the complicated machinery above the stage of the full theatre that go to make the region known as the flies is not our province at the moment and belongs to full-theatre technique but, for completeness, the *Armed Batten* system of curtain hanging will be described here with the other curtain settings, though its use is designed for theatres with flies. By its inclusion we shall continue our gradual progress during which we have seen, first, the curtain set developing its own proscenium of curtains, a system for use in bare halls, then the curtain set for use in halls already equipped with a proscenium and overhead tackle, and finally the curtain set for use in a full theatre with flying-space. These different forms

Fig. 162. The batten lowered for the arms to be swung in and tied before flying.

of curtain set exemplify the way in which set handling is altered to suit the exigencies of various stage conditions. Fig. 161 shows an *Armed-Batten Set*. Here the curtain back is attached to its batten and the sides to their battens, but the up-stage ends of the side-curtain battens are *hinged* to the ends of the back batten. The type of hinge may be the usual strap-hinge, or the specially designed *panorama hinge*, which consists of two separate flaps joined end to end by means of a pair of interlinked rings, one of which is fixed on the end of each flap.

The downstage end of each side batten is attached (most conveniently by a bridle and snap-hook) to a special line from the flies. The border is hung in the usual way from its own set of lines.

Often it is of value to have such a curtain-surround fairly shallow, and to mask-in the downstage limits of the sides with a pair of separate wings consisting of curtains hung on flats, which are braced in place in the usual way. This particular arrangement with separate wings is indicated in the diagram.

To strike such a set, the wings (if any) are run off, the surround lowered on all its five lines simultaneously till the battens are within reach of the stage, the lines attached to the

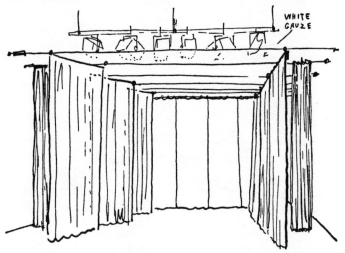

Fig. 163. The Rochdale Curtain Set, hung from a series of strained wires.

downstage ends of the side battens are slipped off and the battens are then swung in (Fig. 162) and folded against the back batten to which they are secured with tyers (or short lengths of rope) and the whole batten flies away up out of sight, with its arms folded upon its chest as it were.

Alternatively, in theatres with a high grid it may be possible to lower only the two lines holding the downstage ends of the side-arms and disconnect them, leaving the sides to hang vertically from the ends of the back batten as it goes up aloft.

The border in any case goes away separately.

144

The last arrangement of the pure curtain full setting that I shall describe is a sort of appendix to the chapter. It is an especially ingenious arrangement designed to suit a certain, small, amateur-built theatre, the Curtain Theatre at Rochdale. It is upon the side-hung principle and is unique in being equipped with a ceiling (Figs. 163-4-5).

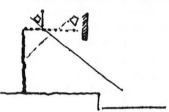

The ceiling is of white net and rests upon the seven or eight strained wires necessary for the working of the set. As the ceiling is of net, lights can be used from above through

Fig. 164. Section of Rochdale Curtain Set.

the net, which is a very unusual arrangement. Its only drawback is that the back curtain of the set must be lit from the Number One batten. On certain occasions a Number Two batten may be used, but the lamps must be shielded with especial care or their lighted vents will gleam through the ceiling net (Fig. 164). The Number One batten lighting the backcloth tends to throw actors' shadows upon it, but the net diffuses the light and if frosts are used, shadows will be nearly unnoticeable.

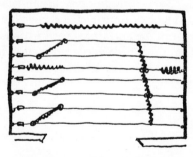

Fig. 165. Plan of Rochdale Curtain Set.

This set is interesting as providing the alternative of hanging the side-curtain strips either edge to edge in a continuous wall or angled so as to form a series of wings.

In the Rochdale method the ceiling of the set is stretched above a number of transverse strained wires. Each of the side-curtain strips is attached to a separate short batten at the top, and the batten is provided with a hook at either end. The hooks can be attached to every other wire (as on the stage left of Fig. 165) when they form a continuous wall, or to every wire (as on the stage right) when the curtains hang diagonally under the wires, and form a succession of wings with, if necessary, the addition of further strips to preserve the depth of the acting-area.

If the strained wires are each provided with a set of rings a traverse curtain for running across the stage can be hooked to any wire and worked between any pair of wings, its gathered-back fullness acting to mask the space left between two wings. Masking the space, it frees the intervening wire for working the traverse rings (see Fig. 165).

The Pure Curtain Setting is really only a method of draping a stage, and, except on occasion, is not used as scenery without the addition of details or a special arrangement or draping of its parts. Its single use otherwise is to provide a perfectly quiet and nearly 'non-existent' background for such a turn as a *pas seul* in a ballet programme, and then only when the number is of a specially abstract nature like 'The Swan' of Pavlova. Such curtains are almost inevitably of black velvet. Its real function is to mask the stage, not to set a scene. It is stage-setting, not scenery. Some people say you can play anything in curtains. That is wholly untrue of the pure curtain set and only partially true of the curtain set used with details of scenery. The Pure Curtain Set is a very restricted style indeed. If you add a detail to the curtains it becomes a Detail Setting and not a Curtain Setting, and that is something very different.

CHAPTER FOUR

Theoretical Interlude,
A Distinction between Stage-Setting and Scenery

SECTION 15

The Existence of a Distinction—Definitions of Scenery,
Setting, Details of Scenery, Full Scenery, Permanent
Set, Standing Scene—Inconsistence of Certain Styles
with Modern Art Theories—An Analogy with Illustration

The term 'stage-setting' is a generic one. It may be justly
used to cover the whole field. This is in a sense unfortunate, it
makes definition difficult, for, if we take the whole field of setting and remove from it so much as is covered by the term
'scenery', what can we call what is left? Popular usage seems
inclined to call it 'stage-setting' still, which of course leads to
confusion, for 'scenery' is also a branch of the larger 'stage-
setting':

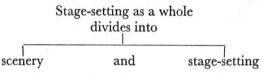

Stage-setting as a whole
divides into

scenery   and   stage-setting

There exists a very good reason, however, why we should
make a distinction here, for *setting a stage* as such, that is masking it, draping it, making it generally fit to receive a show, is a
different job from *setting a scene*, a specific scene in a show, for
which *scenery* of some sort is always essential.

The reason for such a distinction is that it allows us to dis-
sociate scenery from the rest and to see for the first time what
scenery is and that it may be of either of two sorts.

It will help us if we reserve the term 'scenery' to-day for
such pieces as are distinctly made to assist the setting of a
specific scene in a show, and have to be removed and replaced

149

by other pieces in order to 'change the scene'. Scenery is directly related to a specific scene. We may now notice that this term need not cover all that has hitherto been loosely called scenery on the stage, for there may be certain 'pieces', or curtains, or such like, which remain through more than one scene and are not directly related to that scene as a scene, they are rather a general background or a frame or a surround, equally suitable to other scenes. They are 'stage-setting' and not scenery. Scenery must be directly related to a specific scene.

If we grant this we find that scenery may be of two sorts: (1) Full Scenery, where the whole view of the stage, at the back and sides and top, consists exclusively of a group of specialized pieces relevant only to the current scene and all to be removed before the setting-up of the next scene. And (2) Partial or *Detail Scenery* where the scenery is reduced to a single detail (or a few details) upon whose removal alone the stage ceases entirely to represent that scene, and there is left only the surround. It is the *surround*, or accompaniment to the detail, which we call the stage-setting, and this is always of a non-particularized nature—plain flats or curtains or suchlike things—to which there can be, without inconsistency, imparted another atmosphere by the setting in front of another detail of scenery.

We have then in our province:

The general setting of scenes
which may consist of
either

full scenery covering   or   a stage-setting plus
the whole stage,   a detail of scenery.

To set a scene we may *either* use a general stage-setting and particularize it with a detail *or* dispense with the stage-setting, increase the detail in its dimensions and its complexity, until it itself masks and fills the whole stage and is no longer a detail but a full set of scenery. Our subject then is in three departments:

1. The simple general setting of a stage (nearly always with curtains).
2. The use of details of scenery.
3. The use of Full Scenery.

With the third department we must deal elsewhere.

As an aid to making clear this distinction, let us consider the term 'Permanent Set'. As I have suggested, the setting may remain permanently, or with slight modifications, throughout many scenes, and the term 'permanent setting' is quite in order. A permanent set is an arrangement capable of suiting several scenes by the rearrangement of its parts, or by the addition or alteration of details set among or against them. But 'permanent scenery' is something unthinkable—you could not play always in one scene. The scenery must be changeable, though the setting may be what we call 'permanent'.

It is to be regretted that modern usage is so free with the term 'stage-setting', and the reason the distinction I am making now is not more clearly realized rests in the indiscriminate way in which the term is applied to anything inanimate seen upon the stage.

In instance of this confusion I quote this question and answer:

'If a play', someone asked, 'takes place in one scene throughout, and that scene is an elaborate arrangement of realistic full scenery, is that not a "permanent scene"?'

To which the answer, made in all good faith, was:

'No, because "permanent scene" is only applicable to scenery that can be changed for each scene.' This is clearly nonsense and immediately starts the question: 'Then, why is it called permanent if it is meant to be changed? And why am I forbidden to call the other scene permanent purely on the grounds that it is *not* changed?'

This is the state of affairs which is ideal for breeding a general atmosphere of confusion and distrust. It can be put right once and for all by using the proper words:

Obviously the second speaker meant that it was not the scenery that was permanent but the setting. No scenery is ever permanent. It belongs only to its own scene.

And for the first speaker whose show took place in one scene with no change throughout, the term to use would have been *Standing Scene*, which implies something very different from 'Permanent Set'—it simply implies a scene that stands through the whole show.

Now why do I not use the term 'permanent set' in place of the less familiar 'detail set'? Because again I wish to avoid a confusion. There is an essential difference between the two. And though the Permanent Set is a highly-specialized department of theatrical presentation that belongs to Full Theatre technique, its distinction from the Detail Set must be made right away. Perhaps the most famous example of the Permanent Setting in modern times in England is the setting for *The Beggar's Opera* designed by Claude Lovat Fraser. If to this we add the setting by the American, Woodman Thompson, for *Malvaloca*, we shall have two arrangements differing very markedly from the Detail Setting as I have defined it.

In *The Beggar's Opera*, the set consisted of a permanent, built back wall and side walls (with their doors) upon which details of scenery were hung, and changed, to denote the scenes and their transition. In *Malvaloca*, the added details were not painted pieces applied, but additions to, and re-arrangements of, the standing walls themselves.

The characteristic which distinguishes these two examples from Detail Sets is that the walls upon which the changes are rung are far less indeterminate than the silent curtains of the Detail Set that we have so far seen making the surround for the changeable pieces of scenery. The walls are much more elaborate, much more particularized, much more approximating to scenery proper. They are, however, not specialized enough to serve for only one scene. They supply the basis for the whole show—not a general type of show but this show in particular—and are then determinated still further by the addition or arrangement of details specially for each scene.

A Detail Setting, then, is one where a detail of scenery is set against an indeterminate surround. A Permanent Setting is one where the detail is set against a much more sharply determined background, which may, by the rearrangement of its parts, enhance the effect of that detail as a determinant of the scene. So far in this book our concern has been, to all intents and purposes, only with stage-setting in the narrow sense. We have next to see the introduction of scenery. But there is a special point about the nature of scenery (and especially of full scenery) that is the cause for this interlude in our main story. It is that scenery *may* lead us into a profound theatrical error. This is to serve as a forewarning.

The modern world (our own world) has formed a conception of art where the search is for a reduction to essentials and the abandonment of inessentials. With this great vivifying idea of twentieth-century thought all our work has so far been consistent—we have not yet described any setting that has an inessential element. Beyond the limits of this volume, however, are two styles of scenery that may be inconsistent with modern ideas—Backcloth-and-wing Sets and Box Sets. We are going back as we go on.

Go on we must because the cloth-and-wing style and the box style are the two most used forms in the modern theatre. But they are not necessarily by any means the most useful. They are the most expensive, the most troublesome and the most complicated. Properly they demand machinery costing hundreds of pounds for their correct use. And their incorrect use is one of the most serious obstacles to theatrical presentation as a vivid art. It is killing it.

These two forms are the acme and goal of the aspirations of most amateur groups and most professional groups, though their use involves the breaking of the most important rule of the art-theories of the first quarter of our century; it involves the inclusion of inessentials.

Scenery is something without which theatre had progressed perfectly happily for twenty centuries and more, and now a couple of hundred years after its incursion, we are asking ourselves just what we are to do with full scenery. The more progressive movements of to-day, which form the great majority of the movements of to-morrow, reply that they are tired of full scenery. They are seeking to return to some sort of stage-setting. For full scenery involves the use of inessentials.

Let me give you an analogy of what this means in another branch of art which is going through a very similar process and then I can make the distinction between stage-setting and scenery more clearly. The analogy I would give is that of magazine-illustration.

Let us take a typical incident of fiction and see the two strikingly different treatments the old method and the new will give. Let us take an incident with vivid action—a figure striking a blow, a vigorous blow, where the whole intention of

Fig. 166. Story-illustration analogous to a full setting.

the picture is in the vigour of the blow, and where the figure and the object on which the blow falls are the subject of presentation—are all we want to say. Let us suppose a blow with a sledge-hammer upon an anvil, the forging of a sword—or the old fairy-tale testing of a blade by splitting an anvil. Whatever you like.

Here is what you would do in the old style of illustration (Fig. 166).

How much of this is essential? Surprisingly little.

So you have another form of illustration to-day that is composed like Fig. 167.

Those are all the essentials. It is all there.

Now how does this analogy apply to theatrical presentation? The second picture is like the simple detail setting, the first is like full scenery.

You know already the simple ancient form of stage: here it is again (Fig. 168). There may be an entrance through the curtain at the back, but otherwise the scene is characterless, it might stand for anything, it is like a blank page.

Fig. 167. Story-illustration analogous to a 'detail' setting.

It can be 'illuminated', 'illustrated' or decorated in many ways. Fig. 169 shows the ancient Greek manner. The entrance has been moved slightly to the stage-right and is supplemented by a window in the back wall, and several details of pattern, colour and elaboration have been added. Let us pause for a moment at this point. We are still before an unparticularized scene. The door and the window are as yet not so much items of scenery as elements of the stage wall, more or less essential to the practicabilities of the stage.

Says Professor Allardyce Nicoll apropos of this type of Greek mime stage:[1] 'Here we have a "formal setting". There is no indication of change of scenery, but we do possess evidence of the use of what may be called scenic properties.

[1] See *Masks, Mimes and Miracles*, p. 64.

Altars appear frequently, and many important characters are seated on thrones. . . . Noticeable, too, is the laurel-bush. This laurel-bush is represented in several vases . . . and its presence in these would seem to suggest that when the scene was supposed to take place in a grove a single bush was sufficient to create in the minds of the audience the imaginative illusion of the theatre.'

'Scenic properties' is a good phrase. Here is the beginning of scenery. It is at this point that we may return to Fig. 169 and notice now the sinuous branched stalk standing near the window. In such a manner is the laurel-bush mentioned by Prof. Nicoll represented on the vases. We do not forget the

Fig. 168. The 'bare page'
of simple theatre.

Fig. 169. The 'page', firstly
decorated and then 'illustrated'
with a detail setting.

point mentioned by Prof. Nicoll in a footnote continuing the above quotation: 'Although, of course, in Greek pictorial art tradition permitted the introduction of a simplified conventionalism. The Phlyakes vases, on the other hand, are sufficiently "realistic" to allow of the above deduction.'

So now we have a position exactly analogous to our second magazine-illustration. A situation where just as much of the stage or page is occupied as is necessary to set forth in concentrated form the spirit of our presentation. The rest of the space is left blank or is occupied by material not directly re-lated to the scene presented. The rest of the stage apart from this laurel-branch might suit any play. But the laurel determines the whole, the stage becomes a grove.

Notice well, however, that just as in the second magazine-illustration the rest of the scene, the inessential blacksmith's shop, was left out and yet the essential atmosphere was wholly maintained, so here the inessential rest of the grove is not represented, but the essence itself is there to make the scene. Such then is simple scene-setting, and the laurel is the essential detail of scenery.

Now let us turn to the other analogy between the full illustration in a square and full scenery. In full scenery we have the same basic stage but in very different circumstances, not now free-standing but in a theatre-building, and the theatre-building makes a very different thing of the stage; now we must represent it not as in Fig. 168 but as in Fig. 170. Here is no virgin page, suiting any subject, whose space we may occupy as much or as little as we like with as small a concentrate and as essential a summary of our scene as will convey its atmosphere, leaving the rest of the space to be itself—a background and a foil, but all fit to be seen—now we have a *space to fill*. And not, moreover, a blank space. In it is everything we do not want seen. Before we can put on a show we must hide all that which appears behind this new proscenium opening and hide it now with scenery.

Fig. 170. *The very far from bare 'page' of a typical full theatre.*

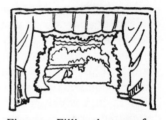

Fig. 171. *Filling the page of a full theatre where the whole space must be filled.*

Fig. 172. *Another example.*

That is one of the functions of scenery—to hide ugly walls. We cannot mask out the undesirable with curtains and set our scene with a detail and an essential for we have given ourselves to the grip of full scenery and the consequence is we must *fill* the space. As in Figs. 171 and 172.

157

Every single inch of this elaborate paraphernalia must be designed and painted differently for every scene. Just as with the story-illustration in a square, *the space has got to be filled*—filled with something or other. The essential is no longer enough. We must design and invent up to the limits of our opening. Piece upon piece must be added. Then all this vast agglomeration of things real and things represented must be swept away in a matter of seconds and replaced by a completely new collection before the show can pass from scene one to scene two, and preserve the vestiges of the unity of presentation—of a show as an evening's whole.

Now he who points out the fault of an accepted method is often mistaken by his hearers to condemn that method out of hand. I do not condemn full scenery, nor the illustration in a square. I merely point out that they include inessentials, that is all I wish to say. That it is often a gesture of richness to include inessentials and to play with them and group them with a lordly competence I fully admit. Nature herself is apparently such a prodigal architect. But there are two faces to her manner. Our age concerns itself with another and in our times economy may be a beauty. For economy shows its prodigality in that which is left unsaid, and the vaster that undesignated territory the more closely may each spectator fit what is seen to his own vision.

To a simple stage-setting, then, you need add no more than the essential of scenery: but in 'full scenery' you are forced to use, at the least, a certain number—and not a small number —of pieces, all of which you *must* include and incorporate in your scenic design, whether the design needs them so far as the scene is concerned or not, and much may be, from the *scene's* point of view, inessential.

Such then is the distinction between stage-setting and scenery. Now wherein does the danger of scenery lie? Whither may its 'inessentials' lead us?

SECTION 16

The Inessentials of Scenery and the Origins of a Mistake—The Rise of Scenery—The Fortuitous Incidence of Perspective—Realism

In the past, a strange state of affairs arose in which the men of the theatre, although possessing a technique by which they could set their scenes with no more than an essential of scenery, adopted a new method and laid upon themselves the obligation of using for every scene a *full set* of scenery with all its parts, essential or inessential as each might be to their scene.

Not only is it in itself worth while to examine this rise of scenery and to note what it superseded, but it is good in that it brings us face to face with perhaps the most serious evil in the setting of shows—an evil by which the show ceases to be theatrical. A reasonable person could scarcely be brought to believe that scene-designers would deliberately avoid making their work theatrical. But so, in fact, it has come about.

The situation arose when the Elizabethan stage sank into oblivion and the first closed-in theatre with a proscenium came to take its place. What was the vast difference between the two methods of presentation—the Elizabethan and the Jacobean? Why did the latter lead to this dilemma? What, first of all, do we know of Elizabethan presentation (which was very close to the principles that I have been discussing up to now in these pages)?

To understand it we must not have our minds biassed by a desire to find on the Elizabethan stage something analogous to the full scenery we know on our own. Some who have gone to the other extreme have pictured the Globe stage as bare to the point of nakedness, with a mere notice hung on the wall as the only indication of a 'décor' of truly fig-leaf sparseness. But we know that is not consistent with the mime's spirit unless he is absolutely unable to afford a single note of finery. Give him a tiny margin of expenditure, and out of it the spangles and the drapes, the bits of decoration and the glittering colours so dear to the mimic heart, and so characteristic of the age-old stage, spring up like flowers in the morning of the year. (Whence, it would not be too difficult to prove, they had their origin.) But these decorations are applied to the stage to make it delightful, not, in temporary fashion, to give it the atmosphere of another place for a scene's duration. The stage as such remains clear for all to see—a background for the players. So far as its decoration is 'setting', it is, in the use of the word, 'setting' in the same sense as 'setting' a table for a meal. It consists merely in 'spreading the cloth', in making things ready and arranging necessary adjuncts and occasional decoration with a knowledgeable hand so that all shall be prepared for a show.

It is not of paramount importance, mark you, what show, any more than the prime consideration in setting a table is of what particular meal it is; the alteration of a piece of cutlery, or the substitution of a breakfast cup for a teacup are the merest secondary details. The prime consideration is that air of cheer and invitation that blesses your first sight and makes you sit down with water in your mouth ready to begin, with all you need before you. The meal comes later to that laid table as the play to the set stage. On the stage, a chest at one side or a table at the other are mere details for a stage-manager, but in the 'setting' of the stage, the dressing of the booth —that is where the theatrical spirit can offer to an audience the prospect of a delectable show and an enchanted two hours.

Full scenery is something quite different. It is an arrangement of a multitude of features of a more or less representational nature that go to make a simulated appearance of nothing more wonderful than the place where the scene is supposed to occur—a realistic or representational picture whose subject is the appearance of the place where the actors would have been standing, were the play real life and not . . . not what? Not merely an imitation.

So by its very nature, purely realistic scenery defeats its own theatrical ends, and by its own existence calls attention to the unreality—to the fake, if you like—of the show.

Such decoration as the mime-stage had was not realistic and was scarcely representational. Those off-shoots of the mimes, the amusement-fair people, in later times set up a roundabout for our delight. They may even come so far up to date (as the mimes are always doing) as to replace the old fine horses with motor-cars, but the decoration of the round-about as a whole keeps all the old roundabout's flamboyance; it never verges on the imitation of an open road for the motor-cars to drive upon. The institution remains, a roundabout, gawdy and fine perhaps, but with the finery put on for its own sake—for fun, not to turn its appearance into scenery for the motors.

The Elizabethan theatre was peopled with mimes and the stage then was frankly admitted as a table on whose surface presentations of certain characters met and acted out an epi-sode or a satire, but the 'locus' of the players' actions was never, even remotely, considered as a thing to be presented or imitated. They said: These are players on a stage, why pretend them to be on anything else? The stage meant enough. The gods were shown to the people—not in heaven but on a stage. And the gods not the scene were what mattered. You could leave it to them to make heaven felt. The stage was just to help you to see them better, and to give them a place to come in on and go out from. And that is precisely what the stage is meant to do.

The decking of the stage then, anciently (though it might be as fine as you like, as fine as is a roundabout at a fair) had not to deal directly with the locus of what was performed upon it. Till the Renaissance this was never closely repre-sented, though it might sometimes be symbolized.

So much for the relation of the *stage-setting* to the Eliza-bethan show. Now what about Elizabethan *scenery*? Yes, it is quite consistent with the above that they might use scenery, but only that 'essence' of scenery, those details about which we have spoken. It is most likely there would be that sort of 'scenic property' that Prof. Nicoll saw on the Greek stage, and thence would come the setting of the atmosphere by means of a detail—after all that was in the mime's tradition, why should they have forgotten? Further, the Elizabethan stage contained both an 'inner stage' and balconies where, provided curtains could be drawn over their openings, there is nothing to prevent our supposing scenery in more or less simple form would creep in—anything to make the show theatrical and there would be the ideal place for the detail!

But when all seemed well with this Elizabethan stage, when it was at the summit of its power and was inspiring drama of unsurpassed quality, there arose—quite suddenly arose out of the blue of the Mediterranean sky—a method by which the scene appeared no longer to be on a stage but in a street. on a mountain, in a forest. The stage was completely disguised with the simulated appearance of another place. This became possible because for the first time the scene was viewed through a hole, like a peepshow, though a far larger hole—no less in fact than the new-born proscenium arch. Instead of a small flat space from which the action might descend and flow, if it pleased, over all the earth, and upon which any 'scenery' had to be a mere detail alone or against a background, we have a vista through an arch, the world is cut off, the place circumscribed. But against its far limits there may be set, to compensate, a painted vista of seemingly infinite extent. And there is the point: not only *may* we have this backing all round our scene, we *must* have it, it is indispensable. When we set no bound to our acting space it mattered little how much of the world lay about it. Now that we put a line around it we must not be allowed to see over that line. A frame sets a limit in more than one sense; besides demarking our picture, it limits our economy. We have now to fill that frame.

With what do we fill it? We fill it with scenery—screens or cloths or curtains. And remember we may not have one piece of scenery here and another there, with, painted upon them, just enough for our requirements as a setting to our scene, as the Elizabethans might. We must *fill* it with scenery so that there are no holes through which the beyond may intrude and distract the eye from our picture. In short, we must mask.

Having then to fill our vista with these masking screens, there arises the question, what are they to look like? And that is the root question of scenery-design. They must be coloured to our satisfaction, but how? To paint them to look like the real spot where the scene is supposed to take place is one suggestion. Why did it gain such an ascendance?

I have emphasized that these 'screens' (or whatever they might be) were introduced to back a vista—a view through a hole. A remarkable and purely fortuitous happening now comes into the question and offers a theatrical problem that has never been solved for three centuries and is at length given up as insoluble. It happened that about this period in history the new science of perspective was charming the renascent mind and being for the first time formulated with tremendous ingenuity. Now, mention a 'vista' to a world brimming with the zeal of discovery and with perspective a new toy: There is little doubt what form the treatment of that vista will take—it will be a perspective treatment.

And so it was indeed. Every early scenery-designer was a perspective-scientist. It follows now (and it is odd to see how far the whole art-world was for centuries involved in the consequences of this simple concurrence) that the designer and master of perspective had to design the manifold elements and planes of his scene not only for a perspective subject but, if he knew his job, the whole must be so 'painted according to the rules' that 'it will appear to him that views it from the point F as a regular piece of perspective placed in A', that is in the plane of the proscenium opening. It is clear where this is leading. We are coming to have for our aim to make beholders see 'a thing which they denied could be done'. From there it is a short step to attempting to confound them with the verisimilitude of the design. And thereafter it becomes a race to reach the most realistic scenery.

The two quotations above are from Andrea Pozzo's learned treatise on perspective dating from the beginning of the eighteenth century. The first quotation is from the letterpress to Fig. 73, vol. 1, the second from Fig. 44, vol. 2. The cryptic 'point F' in the first quotation is very interesting, it is upon that point that a certain seat in the auditorium is situated, the richest spectator's seat, the patron's seat, and only from that single seat can the appearance of the perspective be quite correct. It is increasingly false as you move to the front, to the back or to the side. And that is the trouble about all the marvellously ingenious perspective in the theatre—it is the reverse of democratic—it is not for an audience but for a favoured person. It is never quite perfect save for one man.

Now at length we are indeed trapped. Not only must we include areas of scenery inessential to the scene though necessary for masking, not only must we paint these in key with the rest, but we must make that whole key realistic. These inessentials must look like real things—stun the audience with brilliant verisimilitude. . . . And yet, by their own nature they can never be successful therein, for the more complicated the perspective, the falser it seems from a side seat.

To-day perspective is being abandoned, but realism (encouraged by the box set) remains a little longer, and now it is perfectly true to say that the design of a box set is mostly not a scene-designer's job at all but an interior-decorator's—any such firm could make scene-designs in its drawing office. . . . And scenery then ceases to be very interesting.

Fortunately that stage is beyond our present range, let us return to the business in hand.

The Parting of the Ways: (*a*) Detail Setting, (*b*) Full
Theatre Procedure with Full Scenery—The limitations
of (*b*)—We return to examine (*a*)

We stand now, in pursuit of the technique of theatrical
presentation, at the parting of the ways. On the one hand lies
Stage-setting, the continuation of our simple methods but
with a certain variation—the suggestion of scenery, but a
'concentration' of scenery kept to one detail or so, set skilfully
in any of those backgrounds with which we are now familiar.
On the other hand is the maze of Full Theatre Scenery. Before, we asked only for a stage, and we could present our
show, but here we need, beside a stage, the proscenium arch,
the lighting, the flying-room, the grid, the weights and pulleys of a flying-system and a host of other mechanical complications, or our work can only appear a poor imitation and
so a failure on principle.

If a fully equipped theatre is at hand, then we must know
how to use it, and since the knowledge is wide and various, it
behoves us in another place to study it. But we shall always be
quarrelling with that equipment; we shall find how limiting
it is instead of offering boundless possibilities. We may even
become theatre-fanatics intent on pursuing that elusive system, a perfectly equipped theatre. We may be tempted to
specialize on flying-equipment or on lighting-equipment, and
to study our subject to the exclusion of Theatrical Presentation, becoming mere bores . . . or we may resist that tempta-
tion. On reflection we shall.

We shall find with surprise that on arriving, with a technically well-designed scenery-scheme at a fully-equipped
theatre, it is quite on the cards that we shall be told: 'Ah, you

can't do that on our stage—on that point we can only go so far because of—' and they mention some 'snag' or other, like the curve of a cyclorama, a low fly-floor, bad sight-lines, a raking stage, a low grid, a projecting staircase here or there . . . any of a hundred and one things.

Stage work then becomes hard work—hard in the harried, hampered business-man's sense. Like business, it needs rationalization. It needs scientific handling. To be truly scientific, the handling must be in a scientifically planned theatre. And there is none. Because no one has yet taken the trouble to collect, examine and collate the principles of Theatrical Presentation.

And so it is with special attention that I ask you to consider the Fifth Style or Detail Setting as a form that, in my opinion, is the most useful category of theatrical presentation yet devised. With the Detail Setting we shall conclude this volume and our examination of the first part of setting. Beyond it lies a new territory—the equipment, understanding and use of a theatre-building and scenery. With an idea, now, of its nature and its especial interest let us turn to this style whose possibilities are as wide as anything we may ask of theatre, and only fail us when we seek to be not theatrical but realistic.

CHAPTER FIVE
Detail Setting

SECTION 18

Eight Varieties of Detail Setting: 1, Painted Detail—
2, Built Detail—3, Representational Built Detail—4,
Real Detail—5, Frame Detail—6, Selected Real Details on Special Background—7, Selected Real Details on Fantastic Background—8, Screen or Skeleton Detail

---

A Detail Setting is one where you do not fill the whole stage with scenery.

Instead, against curtains or some other indeterminate surround you station a more or less small piece of scenery which 'sets' an actual *scene* just as the existing surround has already 'set' the stage ready for a theatrical show. To change from one scene to another, the detail must be struck and another

Fig. 173. Detail Setting. (1) A simple set-piece before curtains.

Fig. 174. (2) A set-piece in a centre opening.

detail or arrangement substituted. But throughout the play the surround remains unchanged. Its purpose—to mask-in the stage—is a helpful fundamental of each scene and *reduces the amount of scenery needed to essentials only.*

As an introduction to the varieties of Detail Setting we may enumerate five especially, and add three others which are interesting in being of a family and in making a sort of reversion to the very first types of setting that we discussed.

169

Against the standing surround of the full curtain set with back curtains, side curtains and borders, we may set first of all, as the simplest example, a *painted detail* in the form of a groundrow, a set-piece (Figs. 173 and 174) or a small backing or cloth within a central opening (Fig. 175), or a combination of these (Fig. 176).

Fig. 175. (3) A small cloth in
a centre opening.

Fig. 176. (4) A cloth and
groundrow in a centre opening.

Secondly, we may set among our curtains certain *built details*, which may be *abstract*, non-representational shapes—curved screen-walls or blocks and rostrums (Fig. 177).

Or (third type) they may belong to the vast crowd of *representational built details*, either doors, windows, fireplaces, etc., engaged among the curtains (Fig. 178) or shapes and modelled pieces, free-standing in front of them (Figs. 179 and 180).

Fig. 177. (5) Abstract built
details.

Fig. 178. (6) Representational
built details.

It is with the examination of the simpler 'representational built details' and their construction that we shall find certain evidence we are still seeking to enable us to formulate our final rules for the correct overlap of the strips of curtain, without which we shall not be able to present a workmanlike and neat appearance in our curtain and detail set.

The fourth variety of Detail Setting that I shall distinguish is the *real detail* set, where the detail, set before the curtains, is a real object, a chair, a lamp, a reaping machine (Fig. 181), or the anvil and tent which we have already mentioned in our discussion of symbolized scenery (see Fig. 2).

To the fifth variety I have given the name of *frame detail set*, where the detail generally consists of a pair of pieces of scenery symmetrically placed either side the acting-area and

Fig. 179. (7) Representational
built details.

Fig. 180. (8) Representational
built details.

framing, at the sides at least, the stage-setting beyond (Fig. 182). The especial interest of this form of frame detail setting is that it becomes a most useful formula in certain varieties of Permanent Setting when it is combined with one or other of the first four methods of Detail Setting (especially with a painted set-piece); the frame in that case is painted with a less determinate design and remains permanent throughout the whole show, while the detail beyond, which it frames, is changed in the usual way for each scene.

Fig. 181. (9) A real detail before curtains.

Fig. 182. (10) Frame details.

The remaining three varieties of Detail Setting are all of one family. In form they are especially interesting as going back to one of the first principles we enunciated, yet belonging to the most advanced methods of to-day, and their generic name might be the *Background Detail Set*. The use of this form is capable of the highest theatrical expression, and it is employed by some of the most progressive of our professional producers.

In principle the method is to use certain essential real objects, generally carefully chosen pieces of furniture, and to group these few in a compact space against a small backing in the centre of the acting-area, with the usual non-determined surround beyond. However real the furniture chosen to express the scene of the play may be, clearly the screen behind cannot, in general, be anything but artificial and a convention: at most it is a fragment or a symbol of a wall, so it comes about that we have two sub-varieties of Background Detail Setting in one of which the *selected real details* of furniture, or whatever they may be, are set *against a special background* (Fig. 183) designed solely to show them off and supply a more or less indeterminate atmosphere which the details convert into

Fig. 183. (11) Real details against a special background.

Fig. 184. (12) Real details against unreal background.

a scene-setting (like the setting for Lee Simonson's *The Failures*), and a second sub-variety in which the little background is far more sharply determinated and is fully painted, where the other was generally only coloured (this has a pattern or design upon it and the other has none). As this background is itself of so conventional a nature, it follows that the painting upon it cannot consistently be purely realistic, and hence we have the odd mixture which we may label *Selected real details upon a fantastically painted background* (Fig. 184). Now the oddness of this mixture produces a strange, bitter-sweet pungency that is used with remarkable effect in certain styles of presentation. A perfect example of this is seen in the setting for Komisarjevsky's *Hatter's Castle*, which shows this variety of the style pushed to its fullest manifestation—indeed to the point of borrowing from some of the others.

This borrowing, incidentally, is a characteristic of many of these sets, and you must understand that the classification I am making is to be taken only for its convenience as a scale of reference, not as a system of water-tight compartments.

The last variety of Detail Setting with which we shall concern ourselves just now is a further branch of the Background Detail Setting in two forms that I shall call (*a*) *the Skeleton Detail* and (*b*) *the Screen Detail Set*.

With the Screen Setting in its pure form you are already familiar. Suppose the same thing behind the proscenium of a theatre but before a masking surround of curtain—add perhaps furniture, and you have the Screen-Detail Setting (Fig. 185).

The Skeleton Detail Setting (Fig. 186) arises from this and is a form of setting, generally for an interior, where the doors, windows and perhaps other elements of a room, such as the

Fig. 185. (13) A screen detail.   *Fig. 186. (14) Skeleton details.*

skirting-board, are built and stand in their place on the stage but have no connecting walls between them. They stand alone in space and beyond and through them can be seen the indeterminate curtain surround. This type of set, economical and often especially effective, is of most use generally for certain modern plays presented in a manner that clearly must not be the usual pedestrian realism. That discussion takes us to a somewhat advanced branch of our subject a little too quickly, however; let us return to pick up our tale and pursue it steadily from where we left off, and see what technical notes can be made for the construction and handling of the varieties of details. The 'representational' division of the built detail setting covers a very great deal of the subject and, because the construction of doors and windows (which are the type details of the division) differs essentially from that of the doors and windows used in full-scenery procedure, it will be discussed at length. Moreover, these details will all be useful stock pieces for a group entering upon the territory of the Detail Set.

I shall discuss somewhat briefly certain points concerning the elements of the Painted Detail Set, but I shall have to reserve any consideration of the making of paint and the technique of design and painting until another occasion. And then I shall conclude by considering how these simple built and painted details are used in practice with the curtains in Detail Setting and for that purpose I shall take three plays of different categories and discuss the 'plotting' of all their scenes, and the employment of details to set them, and so introduce you to the very important department of scene-designing that deals with what is called the 'scene plot'. Over constructional details of the 'Abstract' division of the Built Detail Setting we need spend little time for there is nothing that is not built according to standard procedure. Similarly, the constructional technique of the three divisions of the Background Detail will automatically be covered by the treatment of the other methods described.

Details among the Curtains: The Use of Doors and
Windows in Curtains—A Note on Painted Detail Con-
struction, a Rough Method of Framing a Set-piece—
Varieties of Painted Detail

We left our technical story at the question of overlaps and
openings. We discussed some of the types of opening for the
Pure Curtain Set, and have now to cross the border-line into
the Detail Style and consider filling these openings with practicable units of scenery, bearing in mind as we do so that the
principle of the overlap of the curtain-strips still remains to
be formulated.

I mentioned the problem the Lena Ashwell Players faced
when, of necessity playing 'in curtains', they had yet to use
practicable details of doors, windows, fireplaces and other
representational built pieces to meet all the exigencies of the
wide variety of plays they presented.

The Lena Ashwell Players used to play generally in a
Town Hall or a converted Public Swimming-Bath. In some
cases the hall was provided with an equipped stage, and in
others there were the barest essentials for a show—a fit-up
proscenium, four pulleys in the roof above, and perhaps four
ordinary 60-watt lamps hanging down.

The method of setting had to be adequate for the simplest
of these Halls and the whole material of the show had to be
unpacked from the small lorry before the performance, set
up, and dismantled and put aboard again directly the play
was over. They played each night at a different suburban hall.

The method of hanging the curtains was as I have described (Section 12), but the openings were made by standing
certain details—wooden doors or arches, of which there was

a limited choice in stock—among the curtains, rolling up the curtains to make an opening.

The material at hand in these details, which made the stage-setting into scenery, was very much as shown in Fig. 187. We will go into the construction of these later.

Fig. 187. Varieties of Representational Built Details designed to standard widths to fit one, two or three curtain widths.

The important part about these units is that they are made to fit the curtain widths, so as to occupy either one, two or three curtain widths, according to their nature. That means they are all either 3 ft., 6 ft. or 9 ft. wide.

The curtains are put up in the usual way, then the curtain at the place where it is intended to brace a door is rolled up to the height of the door top, the door is set in the opening, and the roll of curtain is left resting on the top reveal of the door.

Let us imagine that a door has to be placed in the centre of the stage-right side curtains. When we examine the particular curtain in whose place we decide to set a door, we shall find that the downstage edge of that curtain is hanging behind—is overlapped by—the curtain next to it, but that the upstage edge of the curtain overlies the curtain on that side. If then we roll up the curtain from the bottom, the downstage edge of the roll will be hidden behind the curtain below as we would wish, but the upstage edge is in front—on

Fig. 188. The difficulty concerning overlap which arises when a strip is rolled. Here, the curtains are seen from the stage side; when the roll is pushed behind its two neighbour strips, the edge of its left neighbour will hang straight but, instead, its right will become twisted.

the onstage side—of the other neighbouring curtain and cannot be tucked behind it without crossing the edges of the curtains and ruining the appearance of the hanging folds (Fig. 188).

In practice then the technique of hanging curtains for a set involves the breaking of the rule, that all curtains must overlap their upstage neighbour, when the curtain is one to be rolled for setting a door or window or other opening. In that case, the edges of the curtain in point must lie behind those of its neighbour on *either* side.

The gap that would possibly show between the upstage edge of the curtain and its neighbour is closed by pinning the overlapped edges of the two curtains to the top corner of the door or window with a drawing pin. Or in the case of a pure curtain opening, by securing the edges with a safety-pin just above the opening.

The rolling of the curtain is done in this way (Fig. 189): A piece of wood like a walking-stick is laid along the offstage side of the bottom of the curtain. The bottom edge is wrapped round it and the curtain is then wound round the rod till the roll hangs level with the door-head. Then, with a safety-pin at either side, the vertical hanging part of the curtain is

Fig. 189. Method of rolling a curtain strip upon a rod, viewed from the onstage side.

pinned through to the outer layers of the roll behind (Fig. 190). The shortened curtain will then stay in place.

Concerning this shortening of curtains there arises a point about which stage managers differ. The normal full-length curtain is pleated so as to hang in folds, but when a length is rolled, the curtain will be smoothed out flat over the rolling rod and when at length it is in its place above the opening its lower part tends to be flat and tightened sideways and so to contrast unpleasantly with the folded curtains at either side (Fig. 190a). On this point there are three schools of thought. Firstly, those who say 'The smoothness cannot be helped, it

is part of the convention. Leave it.' Secondly, those who use
two lengths of lath instead of a rolling rod, and drawing-pin
the curtain-end *in folds* to the first lath (as in Fig. 190*b*), then,
laying the second lath, sandwich-fashion, over the first, they
proceed to roll the curtain as before. This method preserves

*Fig. 190. The roll in place and the curtains pinned to the
door reveals. For clarity the drawing-pin heads are shown but
they should be concealed as in Fig. 190c.*

the folds in the upper part of the curtain right down to the
opening-top, but tends to make creases in the curtain when it
is released for the next scene; it gives, with certain materials,
a bulky bundle, and it wastes valuable seconds on the scene-
change. The third school takes another line altogether: here
two wires are strained along each frame-batten; upon one

wire the curtains proper are hung from rings or hooks, instead of being tied direct to the batten by tapes, upon the
other wire certain short lengths (reaching only to the door-
tops) are hung. When a door
is to be set, the full curtains
are drawn aside on the first
wire and a short length (such
as 2 in Fig. 158) is run along
the second wire behind to fill
the top part of the gap. But
unless one keeps a largish
number of short strips, this
method involves making all
door- and window-tops the
same height. Further, the fit-
up frame must, of course,
always be adjusted to exactly
the same height for each show
else the short strips will be too
high and show a gap above

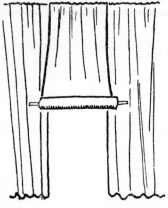

Fig. 190a. A rolled curtain showing
the smoothing out of the folds near
the roller.

the door, or too low and droop over its top. This, when
one has to use one's curtain set on stages of different sizes is a
fatal limitation.

For those companies whose need is flexibility, the arrangement with curtain-strips tied to batten-frame is the best,
with individual strips rolled
to any desired height for
openings. Upon smaller stages
a couple of strips may be left
out of each side to make the
run smaller, and the fit-up
itself pulled up short of its
full height—what extra length
of curtains is not needed is
left rolled or piled at the foot.

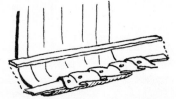

Fig. 190b. Detail of a method of sandwiching the end of the curtain between
two light battens to preserve the folds.

Whatever method of shortening is used, the next step is to
brace the door in the space left (by a method I shall describe
when we deal with the construction of the door), and to secure the loose edges of the neighbouring curtains to the door

frame with such drawing pins as may be necessary to ensure their tidy and discreet hanging.

For pinning rolls, black safety-pins are generally less conspicuous than the ordinary shiny ones. For pinning the side of a curtain to an inset door or window piece, it is neater to insert the drawing pins from the offstage side of the curtain and double back the edge before pressing the pin home in the frame, see Fig. 190*c*.

Finally, I would say concerning overlap that the curtains on the back batten may overlap in whichever way is more convenient, with the reservation that any curtain or curtains which are to be rolled for an opening must be overlapped on *both* edges by the neighbouring curtains.

When we were discussing the making of the curtains, I mentioned that two of the curtains were to be split lengthways to make four narrow curtains. This is the use of the narrow curtains: When it is desirable to set a door in the side, well downstage, adjoining the proscenium, it is generally not desirable to set

Fig. 190c. Diagram of method of hiding the drawing-pin heads.

the door in actual contact with the tabs. To hang a full width of curtain between the proscenium and the door would, however, send the door too far upstage. So we use our half width of curtain, set our door above it, and continue with the usual size strips, putting in the other half of the curtain wherever we find it most convenient. So we complete our surround of curtains, but keep our door well downstage. (We shall see an example of this when we come to discuss *Abraham Lincoln*.) It may also occur that the exigencies of the play demand two doors very close together, or that the size of the stage prevents our allowing the width of a full curtain between two doors. Then again we fall back on our half-width strip and can set our two doors within eighteen inches of each other.

A mantelpiece is set just as a door, save that it stands on the onstage side of the curtains, and not, as the door, behind them. A curtain is similarly rolled up a short way for the opening and a low backing in the form of a two-wing screen is placed offstage to mask the opening of the fireplace, and the electric fire is set in the opening.

So much for an introduction to the placing of Representational Built Details among curtains. Several details of practice remain to be covered but these it will be more convenient to discuss in relation to specific sets in use on a stage and we will put them aside for the moment in order to make a similar brief introduction to the use of the Painted Detail. Then we shall be in a position to devote ourselves to specific practice for the rest of this book and describe the actual setting of three type plays.

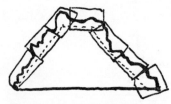

Fig. 191. Simple framing for a set-piece (1) The cut set-piece face down, reinforced at the edges with layers of glued paper.

In the Painted Detail Setting, the whole of the effect of the setting rests in the hands of the painter; upon his design and arrangement of parts around this painted detail, the set stands or falls, while in the Representational Built Detail Setting, where the doors and their shape and arrangement make the set, there is little for the painter.

There can be a drollness and a light-heartedness in this Painted Detail Setting that is not to be surpassed in any other method.

The painted detail is either hung among the curtains so that they frame it, or it is cut out and framed-up and stood before them, forming a 'set-piece'.

The proper construction of set-pieces belongs to the carpentry of full scenery, but there is a way of making a cut-out piece that is considerably simpler. It is a method I have seen occasionally used abroad and, rough as it seems, in practice I have to confess the result is effective.

The design for the set-piece is, in this method, painted upon canvas like an ordinary piece of scenery, either with size-paint (when it can only be rolled for transport) or with dye, when it must be skilfully done, but can be folded like a hand-kerchief and packed in a property-basket.

It is then straightway cut out with a pair of scissors. When the whole shape is finished it is laid face downwards on the floor, and its profile is stiffened as we shall describe, then the whole is battened-out by nailing a frame-work of short light battens behind. The only tools used for the framing-up are a saw and a hammer. No joints are cut whatever.

Fig. 192. (2) *The set-piece face up with the first battens laid under its edges preparatory to nailing.*

The method of framing is merely to nail the canvas through to half a dozen rough bits of wood arranged approximately to the shape of the set-piece and then to turn the whole lot over, face down, on the stage, and nail a couple of long battens over all the lot to keep the bits in place, and there you are!

A stage-hand, skilled in this procedure, sets about the work in this way: As the cut canvas lies face-downwards on the stage, he swiftly judges where his supporting frame-pieces are to come and so can tell what shapes of canvas are likely to project beyond the wood, un-supported. To the back of these he glues two or three layers of brown paper (Fig. 191). He must put a weighted board on these until they dry or they will curl. When they are stiff he turns the canvas face up, lifts the edges and places, underneath them, the battens that are to frame it (Fig. 192), and nails the canvas through to them. The whole affair is turned face down again and the strengthening cross-battens are nailed on the back over the first pieces to hold the whole rigid, as in Fig. 193, where the first battens are left white and the cross-battens shaded.

Fig. 193. (3) *The complete set-piece viewed from behind with the canvas nailed to the first battens (shown white) and the whole stiffened with additional battens (shown shaded) laid over and nailed to the first. The paper has been trimmed to the shape of the piece.*

The piece is then stood up and the brown paper stiffening trimmed to the outline. And in practice it is surprising to see how rigid a shrewdly framed canvas can be.

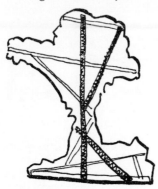

Fig. 194 shows a more irregularly shaped piece, battened out in the same manner.

This framework had (when I saw the method used in Egypt, at least) to stand some harsh treatment, for, as like as not, the manner of bracing it in place on the stage would be exactly like the framing—a rough batten would be leaned against one of the supporting pieces of the set-piece and pinned to it with a three-inch nail, and the lower end of this make-shift brace would be equally viciously nailed to the stage. Each stage-hand carried a very large claw-hammer with a two-foot-long handle thrust in his belt, like a sword, and at the scene-change, he hacked this claw around the nail and wrenched it out again in a split second. How often the stage

Fig. 194. A more complicated piece.

Fig. 195. A small painted cloth as a detail among curtains.

floor needs renewing, or how loudly the orchestra is encouraged to play its *entr'acte* music, I did not enquire.

I think this method of framing is all that could be desired as an example of the 'rough', but it must be admitted it proves equally 'ready', and, in an emergency, when one is greeting a late-arrived, visiting company, whose pieces are not framed out, there is no other method for it.

Our painted detail can take several forms; it may be a

Fig. 196. A small cut-cloth and a backing cloth.

Fig. 197. Two painted flats set at right angles. Such small sets arranged in a central opening in the surround (Figs. 195–8) are often called 'inset scenes'.

simple, small cloth, hung in an opening in the curtains (Fig. 195), or it may be in two planes and consist of a cutcloth across the opening in the curtains and a backcloth behind (Fig. 196). Or it may be two flats set at right angles as in the

Fig. 198. A groundrow-and-backcloth inset.

suggestion for Jessica's house in Fig. 197. It may be a back-cloth with a foreground on a separate groundrow, with the actors playing between the two—as in the bargee-scene in Fig. 198. Or it may be a simple set-piece, either in the middle

185

of the stage with the back curtains closed, or at the back of the stage with the back curtains open and a plain sky-cloth, or a backcloth, or a cyclorama wall behind (Fig. 199). In which case the back curtain may be closed upon it and it can be struck and changed while another scene goes on in front, so avoiding the wait that the dropping of the front tabs brings.

Finally, while these two variants, the Built Detail and the Painted Detail, are still in mind, we may, as we pass, note a third, in which the two are combined, save that the building is much more simplified and much less representational than were our doors and windows.

Fig. 199. A painted set-piece against a sky.

Here the building to be set forth, whatever its nature—house, temple, castle, cottage, stable, boat or bridge—is represented in a brightly painted skeleton that symbolizes rather than reproduces the building itself, see Figs. 200 and 201, where a stable is shown for a nativity play and the effect of two different lightings is suggested.

Such a detail is, in certain circumstances, a perfect feature to hang the action of a scene round. Its artificiality and daintiness help profoundly to create the atmosphere of that other world, the theatre. It is a method suitable only for certain types of show, and somewhat allied to the style of setting in the Japanese Nō plays. The detail set before the non-committal background to make the scene is in those plays a built detail in a much lighter style of building, and is a much more free version of representationalism. It is closely allied also to Symbol Setting, the Detail here is the object, but one conventionally represented against the background.

Fig. 200. A built set-piece for a nativity scene.

In Fig. 202, we turn for a moment to note the simplicity and precise convention with which a boat may be represented on the Japanese Nō stage by an open framework of canes and

Fig. 201. The same lit from inside the roof of the built piece.

ribbons, with a spray of foliage. And, in Fig. 203, how a cottage with a magic gourd-tree at the door becomes four poles and a trellis awning, wound in leaves, with the bottom of the framework padded and wrapped with rag to slip smoothly and silently over the polished stage floor. Fig. 204 is all that is essential of a temple shrine, whose bell summons a lonely wayfarer to its shelter. It is a similar frame with a little roof on top and a small bell within.

The fact that such setting is only suitable for certain styles

Fig. 202. The Japanese style of detail—a boat.

of presentation seems to rouse a strange opinion of it in some people's minds. They say, 'Oh, if it's a method of setting that's not suitable for the typical drawing-room three-act comedy, why consider it?'

Fig. 203. The Japanese style of detail—a cottage.

Fig. 204. The Japanese style of detail—a temple.

The answer is, 'Why *do* a typical drawing-room comedy? I wish you wouldn't!' How eagerly I would welcome some fresh sorts of show. Here is only one of many, many possibilities.

But to elaborate here upon further varieties of painted and other such details will involve us, before we are ready, in the technique of scene painting and the handling of cloths. It will be more to our advantage to consolidate our present knowledge by the examination of the building in actual fact, upon a stage, of the Detail Setting for a show.

For this purpose I shall select types of show which cover a pretty wide ground and introduce us to many technical points of value, and especially types of show answering the most popular and usual demand. True, experimental work and unusual sets form a subject of intriguing interest but they may not necessarily be a help to general procedure and they need to be the product of designers of experience.

We shall then not now attempt to supply the experience of the old hand but, content with indicating that many more applications of Detail Setting than the three we are to examine in detail, are at the command of the designer, we go on directly to discuss the fitting of the set to the show, the turning of the script into theatre, and to review the resources at the scene-designer's call.

Details and Script, 1: An Introduction to the Scene-plot

Up till now we have discussed *things*. But things are not the only necessities of a setting. There must be methods—ingenuities. The application of the knowledge and the use of the things count high. How can we approach that subtler side of our subject, the designer's brain and wits? Perhaps a beginning may be made at that most intimate, most revealing and most rarely understood part of his work which alone among the many sheets of paper he covers in his designing indicates his sense and knowledge of theatrical usage and possibilities as against his other more understandable qualities as an artist-designer. And on that sheet of paper is his scene-plot with the sketch-diagrams beside it.

It is this sheet that we so rarely see, that is so little in evidence at exhibitions of theatrical design, and so rarely neatened, polished up, specially redrawn and framed for public inspection or book-reproduction as the colour sketches of the set or the drawings for the dressmaker may be. These last may become recognized works of art on their own, regardless of what relation they bear to their purpose of making a show theatrical, but always there is left in the portfolio, or handed over to a hurried stage-manager, or tossed aside in a corner, the vital evidence of the designer's quality, his chief claim to greatness in theatre, his scene-plot.

I admit this is not to be wondered at. Mostly the scene-plot is an unengaging scrap of paper—very often the back of an envelope or else a bunch of dog-eared leaves—and it consists of little more than a list of the scenes with cabalistic diagrams of what he hopes to do with each. He is often ashamed of it because it shows his fumbling, his first inaccuracies, and is much corrected. And saddest of all, none but the designer probably can read its meaning. But small as it is, it may contain a week's work and more puzzling out and exercise of wits and wisdom than all but the finished set itself contains. It is from that 'plot' that the pupa of the play emerges as the butterfly of a show.

So far our descriptions of settings and details have been independent of any play. Now, however, we can no longer go on without considering the effect the play has upon the setting, for now we are entering the domain of scenery.

Let us open this new avenue of our subject, which deals with the relation of script to scenery, by considering the nature of the scenery-plot.

So doing, we shall, before we begin to describe the actual construction of specific details of scenery, first consider the method by which the designer arrives at an idea of what details of scenery he wants. When we know what we want, we can go on to consider the best way of making it.

Producers are of two sorts: first, the producers who have, themselves, decided what they want and where they want it; second, the producers who say, 'There is the play, make your plans and tell me the openings and the details so that I may begin rehearsals.'

In either case the adequate co-operation of the two creative workmen, producer and designer, is essential for a unified show. If any doubt exists as to the capability of one of the two, then the other, generally the producer, must take the responsibility for the appearance of the whole show—but in most cases where this happens, the spectacle of the show does not reach that height of interest that it might attain if the two were working, each in sole charge of his own job, and each sympathetically fitting his work in with the other's. Once in a hundred years the two are the same person, and that is the ideal.

In any case (and this is true of any style of setting) the designer's first move is to read the play and *make a scene-plot*— that is, a list, as detailed as possible, of the scenes, and notes (these are important) of any special feature of the scene which the action calls for. Let me give an instance: in Strindberg's *The Father*, the Father throws a lighted lamp at his wife as she stands in a doorway, and the curtain falls on the crash and the sudden darkness. This may be worked by the wife's closing the door on herself as the Father lifts the lamp, so that when he throws it, it bursts against the closed door. If so, then in his scene-plot, the designer *will note this fact*, and make sure that his plans provide for that door being solid in itself, and stably braced, however the rest of the scenery is made.

His attitude of approach at this first reading is important. It should have as its aim the extraction of every particle of matter in that script that is relevant to the setting. The stage directions may contain a great deal, but the text itself may contain equally important suggestions, as we shall see when we consider soon how greatly the dialogue affects the hingeing of a door in *Abraham Lincoln*. Above all the shape of the show must be fixed.

And the second point of the scene-plot is that upon it must be marked the place of the intervals in the performance and their length. This must be arranged with the producer. The importance of noting the point at which an interval occurs is that any long and complicated change of scenery must be arranged to take place only in an act-wait, when the house-lights are put up. All changes between scenes as distinct from acts—that is, changes made, not during, but between, the long intervals, and when the house-lights are still down—must be quick changes, and must be so arranged as to take not a second more than is necessary. So, on the occurrence of the intervals does the method of setting a play to some important measure depend.

Such a list of scenes with notes and with indications of the intervals is the designer's key to the mechanics of the play. He is able to study this and, among other things, he will set himself to work out how much of the scenery he already possesses in the store may be adapted to the new play, and how much will have to be specially made.

I would impress upon all designers the importance of being completely *au fait* with the scene-store, however small it be. And every dramatic company should have a growing store of scenery. It is very sad to hire scenery for every show, and never to work with your own stuff. Your own stuff, simply but specially made, is better than elaborate stuff hired in. It is a good plan to make a series of scale models of every piece you build—a piece of cardboard, cut to the scale of half-an-inch to the foot, for each flat, etc.—upon which notes should be made of the state of the flat, of its sort (door, window, fire-place or plain flat) and of any structural alteration, cutting-down, topping-up or profiling it may receive in the course of different productions so that a glance at your model-slip will tell you the exact condition of the actual piece. Similarly, curtains may be recorded by cutting to size pieces of corru-gated cardboard (such as is packed round bottles) which will represent by the vertical corrugations the folds of the gath-ered curtains.

The designer has then only to spread his bag of tricks on the table, choose and arrange the elements to suit his play and he can at once see what he has in hand and what he must order to be made. These model units of scenery may be set up in place on a table with the help of lumps of plasticine or by wooden blocks glued behind. A model set so made can also be of great assistance, if looked at through a proscenium arch cut in cardboard to the same scale, by showing the perspec-tive of the different objects from various seats in the house, and the general adequacy of the design in respect of masking.

Very useful scale representations of furniture may be made by drawing the silhouette of the piece on card and cutting it out, taking care that the flap you leave at the bottom to help the piece to stand should be an accurately sized and shaped scale plan of the original. You will then be able to recognize, at once, how much space the piece will take up on the stage, and you will avoid the blunder of an arrangement of furni-ture pleasant on your model but hopelessly congested on the stage.

Such models of units are of great use to the producer as well as to the designer, giving him an idea of the sort of space he can mark out for his actors in rehearsals, and it is a point worth noting that, once the dimensions of the ground plan of a set are fixed, it is well to chalk out on the rehearsal floor, or to mark with tapes, drawing-pinned down, an actual-size plan of the proposed set. The furniture, or substitutes for the furniture, can then be arranged and you have a chance to decide whether the space you have estimated will prove adequate or no, and whether there are any odd corners of the set where the sight-lines will prove difficult and where the producer must avoid placing any action vital to the plot.

The chalk lines need not be made necessarily for each rehearsal, but should be used once or twice early, before the action of the play settles down.

It may be useful to mention, with regard to masking, the following point that is not always recognized: a thing is masked from all that part of the audience that you cannot see when you are standing where that thing is. To ensure then that a door-backing, say, masks, without going down into the auditorium and looking at it from various parts of the house, stand behind the backing and look round its edge. If you can see, through the opening it backs, any seat in the auditorium, then from that seat the backing does not mask.

Whatever part of the audience you can see from the stage can see you.

Details and Script, 2: The Birth of Three Specific
Shows—1, *Abraham Lincoln*

In this section we close in upon the actual practice of our
subject and encounter some passages of cardinal importance.
In it we are going to do something far more interesting than
pay a visit behind the scenes; we are going to pay a visit to
the inside of the head of the presenter of a show while his
mind is working upon the plotting and shaping of his job.

Let us suppose we have to set a play in which the psychological side of the setting is especially important. Let us suppose circumstances require it must be played in curtains, but
the nature of the play demands a realistic atmosphere. It is
a serious play, a longish play, and one concerning which the
producer says of the setting: 'I don't want it to be a "decorative" show, because it fails entirely if it is not a play of ordinary, human people in the surroundings of the everyday
world. I can't see my way to bringing the characters in
through mere openings in the curtains, they have *got* to come
through ordinary doors: they have *got* to see out of ordinary
windows, or the flavour of the play is too rarefied and the point
removed too far from us.'

Abraham Lincoln, by John Drinkwater, sets a good problem
under such conditions as these. Let us see how it might be
solved.

First of all the designer takes the book of the play round to
his studio, and in a leisure evening comes to terms with it,
and this is what he might make out of it in the form of notes
and ideas. If producer and designer are one and the same it
makes no difference, the designer part of him works as follows.

The producer's point that the play would fail if it were set

195

in a 'rarefied' atmosphere may be a little difficult to grasp. What was his idea?

Now in the opening of the play, in the script itself, is a passage that throws a great deal of light on the producer's words, but before reaching this the designer has had to make his first note, for the opening page of the script is a dialogue between two Chroniclers, and there is no stage-direction as to their locality, preceding their lines.

Clearly, they must have somewhere to speak, and so the first note is: 'Chroniclers'.

And now comes the passage which illuminates the producer's point and sets the key of the designs:

> ' *Kinsmen, you shall behold*
> *Our stage, in mimic action, mould*
> *A man's character.*
>
> *This is the wonder, always, everywhere—*
> *Not that vast mutability which is event,*
> *The pits and pinnacles of change,*
> *But man's desire and valliance that range*
> *All circumstance, and come to port unspent.*
>
> *Agents are these events, these ecstasies,*
> *And tribulations, to prove the purities*
> *Or poor oblivions that are our being. When*
> *Beauty and peace possess us, they are none*
> *But as they touch the beauty and peace of men,*
> *Nor, when our days are done,*
> *And the last utterance of doom must fall,*
> *Is the doom anything*
> *Memorable for its apparelling:*
> *The bearing of man facing it is all.*
>
> *So, kinsmen, we present,*
> *This for no loud event*
> *That is but fugitive,*
> *But that you may behold*
> *Our mimic action mould*
> *The spirit of man immortally to live.*'

'So', the designer might say to himself before such poetry, 'the events are unimportant; the man matters. The settings then need not be highly localized, but must present the details of ordinary life so far as they affect a man's movements.' It is more important to throw up the figures of the drama in their march through events than to provide an atmosphere of America in the second half of the nineteenth century.

'I have to use', he says, 'doors and windows, because to surround these real figures with a heavy curtain only and make their entrance a fantastic one, in that it is through a parted curtain and therefore a 'theatrical' entrance, must serve only to make less real their ideas and feelings. No, they go in and out by doors in the normal way; they are limited as we are, by the constrictions of daily life. I must therefore have windows and doors in the curtains.'

He continues reading, making his notes as he goes, and at length when he has finished the play this is what he might have on his paper:

THE CHRONICLERS

Scene 1. Lincoln's Parlour. Early in 1860. A farmer and a storekeeper are sitting, smoking, before fire.

Early spring. Dusk, but curtains not drawn.

During scene, *Susan*, a servant, lights candle and draws curtains.

Map of the United States hanging on the wall.

There is a cupboard. And a drawer.

Stone offers to open the window.

A group of four people come in to *Lincoln* and sit round a table. (So 5 chairs.)

Curtain.

THE CHRONICLERS

Scene 2. A year later. The Secretary of State's room at Washington. He is at table with two men (so 3 chairs).

Knock at door.

Several through scene. (This scene could not properly be played without doors.)

Lincoln enters (so 4 chairs).

Waste-paper basket and bell.

Lincoln asks a messenger to wait in a side room (so 2 doors).

Secretary looks through window into street.

Consultation. Eight men round table (so 8 chairs).

Map on wall larger than in Sc. 1.

THE CHRONICLERS

Scene 3. Two years later. Reception room at White House.

Mrs. Lincoln writing (so chair and table). Bell.

Mrs. Blow enters and sits (2 chairs).

Mrs. Otherly enters and sits (3 chairs).

Lincoln enters and sits (4 chairs).

Quarrel scene. Door for Mrs. Blow's exit; query, opening which way?

Visitors and *Lincoln*, so 2 doors.

Susan lights lamp and draws curtains. Window not otherwise mentioned: can omit if necessary.

THE CHRONICLERS

Scene 4. Cabinet meeting at Washington.

(We might by licence, use the same scene as Secretary's room.)

Seven seats round table.

Quarrel scene. Door opening on? Same door as *Mrs. Blow's*?

THE CHRONICLERS

Scene 5. Evening. A farmhouse near Appomattox.

General Grant and *aide-de-camp* seated at table (3 chairs).

An *Orderly* writing in a corner.

One door. Candle. Bench.

THE CHRONICLERS

Same as Scene 5. Dawn.

THE CHRONICLERS

Scene 6. Evening in a theatre Lounge.

Doors to three boxes are showing.
The 'act' finishes. Doors open.
Lincoln and four others in centre box.
The other two boxes empty into lounge.
Conversation. Speech. Next act called.
Return to seats and doors closed.
Booth enters, opens door, fires and exit.
Doors open.
Curtain.

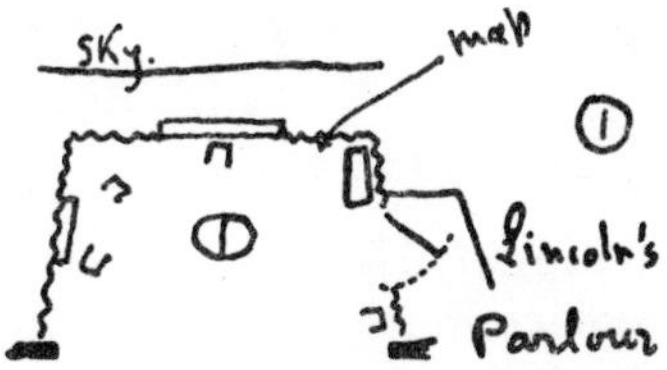

The designer now embodies these stage directions in a series of scene plans and sketches; the plans which he makes first, beside his description of the scenes, will be re-

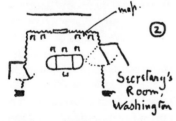

Fig. 205.

vised as he develops the whole and co-ordinates the parts, but a brief summary of his results in this direction might be the group of notes suggested in Figs. 205 to 209 and 212 to 216. Here he now has something he can discuss. He will, for instance, after simply dismissing the Chroniclers to a place in front of the Tabs, have to settle such points as: the door on the stage-right must be well downstage or the two dramatic exits (Mrs. Blow's in Sc. 3 and Hook's in Sc. 4) may be lost in the masked corner upstage. Now if the door is set low down, is it possible to have the fireplace of Sc. 1 low down also? Because it could then be stood in the same curtain as, in the next scene, takes the door. If that cannot be arranged and the fireplace needs to be in the centre of the stage-right wall, certain difficulties will arise in regard to the overlap of two neighbouring curtains for the curtain in which the door is to be set and the adjoining upstage curtain in which the fireplace might be set cannot *both* hang behind their neighbours at both edges as they should. There lies a considera-

Fig. 206.

tion of the utmost importance. You must have a thorough understanding of the problem involved here.

If the producer decides that he must have the fireplace in the centre of that wall, the designer has still a way out by set-

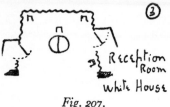

Fig. 207.

ting the mantelpiece in front of the curtains and *not rolling* the curtain behind the fireplace as is usual. He pins the curtain to the back of the mantelshelf and merely pulls it out thence and drapes it over the fireplace backing like a tent roof. This is an efficient arrangement if the door and fireplace must be in different curtains. We assume that they are to be in the same curtain and the designer proceeds with his planning.

If, after careful weighing up, he decides finally the plans of the scenes as shown in Figs. 205 to 209, he might make a diagram as in Fig. 210, whereon he could work out his curtain widths. On

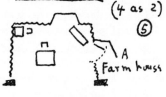

Fig. 208.

this, the placing of the stage-left door offers no difficulty, it is in the second full curtain from the front. The stage-right door is brought nearer downstage by the use of one of the

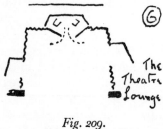

Fig. 209.

special narrow curtains. But this means that the lengths of the two sides of the set will now be different, and, as circumstances demand (he foresees) the use of all three of his other narrow curtains in the back wall, he solves the inequality of length in the sides by carrying the upstage curtain on the stage-left *beyond* the back curtains for half its width.

Now, his difficulty in the back curtains is that not only does he wish to have a three-feet-wide window set centrally therein for one of the scenes, but also a six-feet-wide door, stationed centrally, for another. How is that seeming impossibility to be arranged so far as the widths of curtain are concerned? He does it by hanging a full three-foot width of curtain in the centre (that, rolled, takes his three-foot window), and on either side of this central curtain he hangs a narrow 1 ft. 6 in. curtain, and then *all three rolled* will make a central six-foot opening for his large central door.

The cottage bay-window is, in size, in between these lengths; it is 4 ft. 6 in. across, when set in place. He puts it then

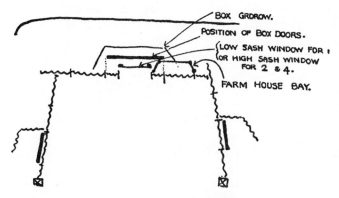

Fig. 210. The places of the details.

to left of centre to occupy the stage-left-hand 1 ft. 6 in. curtain and the adjoining three-foot strip beyond.

If, as is likely, his space in the back wall is now almost used up, he must content himself by hanging the last of the 1 ft. 6 in. strips of curtain between the bay-window and the stage-left corner of the set, and balance the stage-right corner (as his narrow lengths are now used up), by overlapping the right-hand full strip of the back wall beyond the stage-right-side wall of the set, as he overlapped the left side on the back.

This is a specially chosen example of some complexity, which is useful in explaining a way out of the difficulty created when full curtain widths, used alone, dictate the positions of details on a small stage. With a carefully planned use of narrow strips as well as full-width strips, a much nicer flexibility can be attained.

But in an arrangement so flexible, correct overlap will, of course, present some difficulty, and in Fig. 211, a solution is offered, which, however, is still one remove from perfection. At the point marked 'N.B.' the rolling of the bay-window curtains (a wide strip and a narrow strip) will inevitably cause a twist of edge when the roll is tucked behind the central full-width curtain of the back wall.

Such a twist of edge in the back wall is less serious than in the side wall, where the eye is striking sideways and can more easily see through, and so we may, after noting that extra care must be taken to see that the twist is as neatly disguised by pinning as possible, let our plan of overlap go at that.

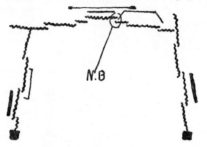

Fig. 211. The Overlap Plot.

With regard to backings, notice that the designer has here simplified the window-backings by adopting the convention that the windows in all scenes shall be in the back wall, and so may all be backed by a cyclorama, or a skycloth and all entrances shall be in the sides, so that it is only the backing of these side-doors that he has to consider. However, regarding the side doors, there is a much more important question to be answered: In which way shall these doors open? On or off? And up or down?

In the first scene you will see that if the door which is on the left, is made to open on and up (as indicated in Fig. 206 and the reverse way to that shown in Fig. 205) it would mask the cupboard and interfere with certain movements. Though we realize that in a normal room all doors open inwards, or in stage-parlance, open 'on', we often have to take stage-licence with this arrangement.

In the second scene, where the long table is used and space further occupied by chairs at the head and foot, the opening 'on' of the left door would again be a nuisance. The stage-right door is sufficiently low-down-stage to clear in any case.

In the fifth, the farmhouse scene, this left door would mask and hinder the setting of the bench where Slaney's excellent little scene is played.

Therefore this stage-left door should be designed to open off.

But there is a point of great importance concerning the door on the stage-right in Scene 3, and that arises out of the exit of Mrs. Blow.

There is a very similar situation at the exit of Hook in Scene 4—so similar in psychological import, in fact, that it might be good theatrical symbolism to have the two events occur at similarly placed doors.

What does this mean? What important point can lie here? Please consider this carefully. It deals with Presentation, and with how the arrangement of even a single pair of door-hinges may make all the difference to putting over the footlights certain scenes of the show.

This is how it comes about: Nearly at the end of Scene 4 there is a quiet but bitter quarrel between two men in a council chamber over the conduct of one of them in an affair of state. They are Lincoln and Hook. Hook is dismissed, unexpectedly, and with some element of bravery by the other—Lincoln.

His career is cut short in the fullness of his pride and he goes, crushed, but with a high head and a sneer on his lips. It is a moment that matters. Simply that. Now if at such a moment, Hook has a fumbled exit to close his final walk clear across the stage, only one who knows the theatre with sympathy can realize to what an extreme the scene is spoiled.

'Hook,' cries Lincoln, as the other reaches the door in a still fury, 'Will you shake hands?' Hook halts a moment, gives a look—'I beg you will excuse me'—and then steps out.

And if he leans forward, grips the door-knob, pushes the door away from him, and steps through in that semi-crouching position—well then, you just have to go on with the play, that is all.

But what if the door is set to open the other way, 'on and up' as the master-carpenter has it? Now Hook can make his drama and the whole atmosphere is left completely different, quivering, electrical, for Hook, at his turn on the heel, gives a

Fig. 212. *The first scene, Lincoln's Parlour.*

very different look, since he knows now that what is coming will be effective, and he hasn't by any means done his scene yet (as he would if the door opened off). Yet his variation is so slight. He merely holds himself very erect, as straight as a ram-rod, then reaches and seizes the handle, pulls the door *towards* him, with a gesture every inflection of which can be seen, because he is well on-stage, and so can make its effect on the audience, looks out, for a split second, 'into the darkness', with the open door a background to his profile. Then, disdainfully lifting his chin, he goes!

Leaving, as his only retort, the door open.

Such a change in the hinges can result in an almost frenzied reaction on the part of the audience, even though (as we hope may be the case) the vanished Hook may hold them completely spell-bound in silence, and the excitement is only in the wide-open eyes and in the tense pulse beats.

The moment passes.

Lincoln is suddenly remembered

Fig. 213. *The second and fourth scenes, the Secretary's Room.*

—he should 'give' that exit entirely to Hook and suppress himself completely until his next movement—when he goes across wearily, all tension sapped, and, humbly almost, shuts that door.

Still keeping the atmosphere, he calls his secretary—'I am rather tired to-day,' he says. 'Read to me a little.' And then, taking the words from the reader's mouth, he says, 'These our actors . . . as I foretold you, are all vanished, and like the baseless fabric of this vision . . . the cloud-capped towers, the gorgeous palaces. . . .'

Slowly, ineffably, the curtain floats down like a feather. That is the moment when the exit of Hook will have its reward in applause.

Had the hinges been the other way, it would have been perfunctory clapping. So it follows, Theatrical Presentation *is* a Job. There *is* something in it.

Fig. 214. The third scene, Lincoln's Reception Room.

However, for us it is sufficient to make us resolve that in spite of the fullness of the stage with furniture, the down-right door will open on and up.

If that were not in itself sufficient, the little passage in Scene 3 would clinch the matter. The childless Mrs. Blow

Fig. 215. The fifth scene, the Farm.

begs Lincoln at the tea-table to go to war. She likes war; she sneers at, and wounds, the bereaved Mrs. Otherly, whose son's death is fresh in mind. Lincoln rises as she goes, puts all the reproof in the world into a quiet but burning speech, and concludes pointedly, 'Good afternoon!' opening the door as he speaks.

What a climax he can make of that 'Good afternoon!' if he can reach out a long arm, and, opening the door towards him, stand by its edge with blazing eyes. But what a difficulty is in his way if he has to lean out and thrust the door offstage, then recover his commanding posture, then get rid of his desolating 'Good afternoon'.

These are some of the factors that have a bearing on door-hinges and upon the Art of Theatrical Presentation.

Fig. 216. The sixth scene, the Theatre Box.

Turning back for a moment to the plans, the designer might set them up to have very roughly the appearance shown in Figs. 212 to 216. Here the essential elements and their positions are indicated, though the furniture is in some cases reduced to save confusion in the small drawing.

In order to get these elements, furniture as well as details of scenery, properly listed, he makes another 'plot' as follows:

	Chairs	Doors	Windows	Tables	Miscellaneous
Sc. 1	5 (simple)	1	1 (sash)	1 (small)	1 bookcase-cupboard 1 fireplace and back-ing 1 small map
Sc. 2	8 (official)	2	1 (high)	1 (large)	1 large map 2 door backings
Sc. 3	4 (simple)	2	0	1 (small)	1 sideboard
Sc. 4, same as Scene 2.					
Sc. 5	3 (rustic)	1	1 (cottage bay)	1 (rustic)	1 desk 1 bench
Sc. 6	5	1 pair double doors	0	0	1 ground-row

REDUCED BY JUDICIOUS DOUBLING TO THE FOLLOWING TOTAL:

Chairs	Doors	Windows	Tables	Miscellaneous
5 simple 8 official 3 rustic	2 single 1 double	1 sash 1 casement 1 high	1 extending with round ends 1 simple square	2 backings 1 bookcase 1 fireplace 1 groundrow 2 maps 1 bench
16 borrow	3 make	3 make	2 borrow	Borrow: bench Make: bookcase fireplace groundrow maps backings

SECTION 22

Details and Script, 3: Constructing the Details—
Doors, Windows and Fireplaces

With his requirements now thus plotted, the latitude
through which the designer has to steer is no longer a vague,
unknown sea, but is in some sense charted. He knows what he
wants. He wants to make certain individual details of scenery,
and to fit those and his curtains together, so as to make of the
two—the determinate details and the indeterminate curtains
—settings for specific scenes.

Let us consider the construction of the details. In the list,
they consist of three door-pieces (two simple doors with their
screen-backings and a double door), three windows (a sash
window, a senate-room window and a cottage bay-window),
one special bookcase, one mantelpiece and one groundrow
for the theatre box.

Let us begin by discussing in some detail the general design
for a simple door to be set in curtains. There are two points to
be made by way of introduction. One—certain people condemn, and, as we have admitted, with some justice, the use of
doors in curtains at all. We agree with their views, but after
consideration have decided that we have to have practicable doors. Our problem then is so to construct and set a door
that it avoids as many as possible of their objections and fulfils as many as possible of our theatrical needs.

The second point is that, having settled that controversy by
arbitrary decision, we must at all costs avoid that particular
fault in our door which, above all other things, makes for dis-
gustingly poor and pathetically amateur showmanship, and
so weights the balance in favour of the curtain purists. That
fault is the using of a flimsy, rickety, jamming, waving

erection, that would be disdained as a 'prop' even by a troupe of music-hall comedians of the lowest and vulgarest comedy, because, though it may be funny, it is quite undependable, a flap that the actors are consistently attempting to open the wrong way, so that they ruin their exits and entrances by feverish alternate pulling and pushing, while the hinges strain and crack, and the whole structure, door and frame, twists on its braces and waves the curtains attached to it, and may—I have known it happen, and particularly on one occasion in the early days of a certain vigorous young man who later became a well-known playwright—end by bodily leaping forward and collapsing on the stage to the complete disruption of the wall of curtain—and the sweating discomfiture of some actor in the scene who rushes to the rescue and mightily lifts up, and holds in place, the creaking structure, till at length the fall of the curtain gives him respite, and the door is again braced in place by the stage hands.

I make no apology for dwelling at some length on the flimsiness of doors in curtains, because it seems to have become a tradition that such doors are not worth worrying about. All the rest of the set may be not only efficient but distinguished, yet the door in the curtains is so often weakly built and wrongly designed. In a dramatic festival of some pretensions, in which some of the most famous of the amateur companies of England were playing, and where some of the most competent and advanced exposition of the variants of Detail Setting were to be seen, one member of the audience was so disgusted by the complete inconsistency and inadequacy of the doors that he suggested taking a collection to provide the theatre with the means of acquiring one decent door—bitterly offering to start the fund with a personal contribution of two shillings and sixpence!

But will his gesture have any effect? Will the theatre go even so far as to fit its own doors with sill-irons instead of the inexcusable three-inch-high bottom rail, that every actor has to remember if he is to avoid tripping up at the threshold, and, even then, must so negotiate that his legs move, on his exit, as if he were going upstairs and stepping over the cat!

Another ugly and inconsistent makeshift, whose only effect is that of slovenliness, is the bracing of a full-sized door-flat in the wall of curtain, omitting a complete curtain from the run where the door occurs—and, as like as not, the flat covered, above the door, with wallpaper.

There are certain rare occasions where this method is used with design and consistency, but in all other cases it is a perfect pointer to the state of mind that doesn't realize that setting matters—whose owner would walk complacently down

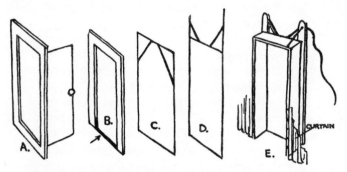

Fig. 217. Points concerning the construction of a door for use with curtains.

Piccadilly in a morning-coat with lavender waistcoat, tweed trousers and a bowler hat.

Let us return to the subject of setting.

A good construction for a door to be used in curtains is as follows: in Fig. 217*a* is shown a square frame of 3 in. × 1 in., with a door hinged to it. This is our starting-point. The construction of the door frame should offer us no problems and we could go ahead and make some sort of a door on the lines indicated in *a*. But there are some improvements. The first is to remove the obstacle of the bottom rail: to do this we omit it altogether and use in its place a *sill-iron*. The sill-iron (shown black in Fig. 217*b*) is no more than a 1 in. × ¼ in. strip of wrought iron long enough to span the opening and provide some nine inches or so beyond at either side to turn up, in which holes are drilled for screwing to the sides of the door posts. (This particular type of sill is more correctly called the *reveal sill*.)

But this tends to lessen the rigidity of our frame. Were it a flat we could brace it by cross-corner braces but as the space inside the frame is to be an opening, clearly we cannot cross it with braces as is suggested in *c*.

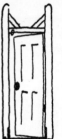

But we can externalize the braces. That is to say, we can prolong the doorposts upward and set the braces across the upper corners, between the extended sides and the top of the door head. As in *d*.

Amateurs often neglect to put reveals on doors. They think it sufficient to hinge them flush with the wall, but a series of doors flush with curtains may have a 'thin' look so that it becomes better to have some of them inset six inches or so, and showing a *reveal* or 6 in. thickness piece (Fig. 217*e*). Not only is this thickness in itself an advantage to the general appearance, but the ledge formed by that reveal above the doorhead is most convenient to lay the roll of shortened curtain upon.

Fig. 218. A simple door shown partly open.

For these reveals we hinge a 6 in. or 9 in. floor-board to either side and to the top of the frame, and perhaps drill the top of one of the styles so as to pass a line through for attachment to the upper reveal (*e*). With this trick-line we can fold back the top and, with our hands, the sides, so that our door piece will pack flat.

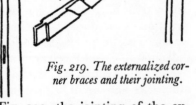

Fig. 219. The externalized corner braces and their jointing.

Fig. 218 shows a simple door without reveals, and Fig. 219, the jointing of the externalized braces.

The door itself consists of a framework of 3 in. × 1 in., generally with a centre rail and a diagonal brace (which must slope *up* from the hinge side, so as to prevent the door from dropping out of the square (Fig. 220).

This frame may be canvassed (in which case the members of the frame must be properly jointed) or covered with ply,

CANVAS.

Fig. 220. *A canvassed door to open off only.*

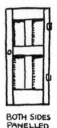

BOTH SIDES PANELLED

Fig. 221. *A double-sided ply door.*

Fig. 221 (in which case they may be merely butt-jointed and secured with 'acme' or corrugated nails, see Fig. 222).

A pair of double doors and a pair of French windows of exactly similar construction are shown in Fig. 187.

Fig. 222. *The use of corrugated, or 'acme', fasteners.*

For bracing a door an extending brace is used (see Fig. 223) of 1 in. square ash, in two sections, connected by metal collars so as to slide upon each other. Upon one of the collars is a set-screw for fixing the pieces at the required extension. At the top end of one piece is a hook to engage in a screw-eye at the back of the scenery, and at the bottom of the other a foot.

These feet may vary in pattern. In Fig. 223 we have an angle of strip metal, part screwed to the brace and part bent back and pierced. Through the hole in this flat piece, a stage-screw (a murderous-looking screw provided with a triangular handle, Fig. 223, top left) is screwed into the stage. Occasionally this turned-back strip is curved, not turned sharply, and is pierced with three or four holes, so that the brace can be set at various angles, and the most suitable hole may be chosen for the stage-screw.

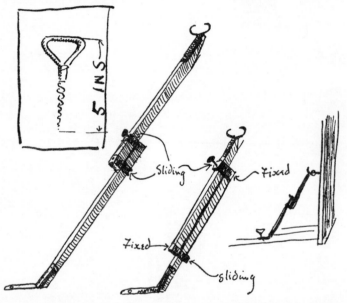

Fig. 223. The extension brace, with a stage screw.

But fixtures into the stage floor may be undesirable or prohibited, and so another form of brace foot, with a turned-up end, is obtainable over which (as in Fig. 224) a brace-weight (or a couple of braceweights) may be placed. These weights will probably have, on their upper and lower surfaces, corresponding projections and recesses, so that a number can be fitted together one above another in use. Fig. 225 shows a weight used temporarily on a plain foot with the slit in the weight riding round the brace.

As a braceweight may weigh round about 28 lb., the cost of carriage on a number of these is considerable, and in many cases it is possible to cast them locally out of scrap iron, or to use in their places sandbags, or even to cast them out of concrete.

Miss Padman tells me that home-making is simple. Drive through the side of a large cake tin or toffee tin half a dozen longish nails at intervals in the circumference. These will become embedded in the concrete and serve to prevent it pulling out of the tin case. Next stand a strip of 1 in. wide iron (flat) about 18 in. long and with

Fig. 224. *A brace with a special end for use with a braceweight to obviate the need for stage screws.*

its lower 5 in. bent at right angles like the foot of an L in the bed of the tin with the upright of the L close against one of the sides. This L is to serve as a handle to help pick up the weight and it serves this purpose still better if the top two or three inches of the stem be turned over outwards to form a lip around which one's fingers can be curled. After these few preparations it only remains to add enough water to a mixture of sand and cement to make a fairly stiff cake and fill the tin therewith. This sets and gives you a reasonably heavy small braceweight.

Fig. 225. *A braceweight used on an ordinary brace foot (only to be considered as a temporary measure).*

In bracing a door the point exaggeratedly made in Figs. 227-8 should be borne in mind. A doorpiece should normally be braced upright (Fig. 226). If it leans, the door will either swing open when it should remain closed (then the piece is leaning towards the side the door opens, Fig. 228) or will insist on closing of its own accord, however much the situation in the play demands it should be left open (then the piece is leaning towards the other side, Fig. 227).

If a piece leans towards the side to which the door opens,

Fig. 226. A door braced upright.

the door may, at its fullest swing, scrape its outer corner on the stage (Fig. 228). The remedy is, if the door opens on, to shorten the brace at the back by means of the set-screw, or tap the bottom of the piece with your foot from behind so as

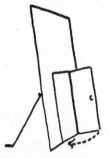

*Fig. 227. A door-flat
leaning back.*

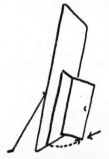

*Fig. 228. A door-flat
leaning forward.*

to knock the lower edge farther onstage. If the flat leans the other way, lengthen the brace, or knock the foot slightly off-stage from the front.

These rules apply of course from another point of view; that is, if you desire a door to fall open and refuse to remain closed, unless actually fastened, then tilt your piece slightly in the direction the door opens, and *vice versa*.

A door in the back wall of a set on a raked stage will often present immense difficulty in this regard, and in the end force the stage manager to have it controlled by invisible trick-lines before it will stay where it is left.

The method of bracing doors is borrowed from full-stage procedure, and was evolved to secure 18 ft. flats in place. It has certain disadvantages, when used with short, light door-pieces, in that the very lightness of the piece imposes so little pressure on the lower edge where it stands upon the stage that an accidental kick on the foot of the door-post is liable to have it over, the brace indeed acting as a fulcrum in aiding this turn. And so two modifications are possible; either the use of a tall triangular French brace (like that on our 'first piece of scenery') instead of the separate extending brace, hinged to either door-post, or the simple little safety precaution illustrated in Fig. 229. Here, to foot of door-post and to bottom of brace are fixed screw-eyes, and dropped in between these is a length of wood (extensible like the brace if necessary) provided at either end with a hook.

Fig. 229. The foot-brace, a safety measure. Above is shown an extending foot-brace for use with flats, below, a simple adaptation for use with a plain door.

This effectively prevents any displacement of the bottom edge of the door with regard to the foot of the brace, and as that foot is secured, by weight or stage-screw, the door is firm.

The remaining details needed for our preliminary play of *Abraham Lincoln* are indicated in Figs. 230 to 236 and with the knowledge we have of the construction of the door, the figures practically explain themselves.

The frame of the sash window (Fig. 230A) may be of 6 in. × 1 in. if preferred, to give a wider surround, and the thickness-pieces (Fig. 230B), are then added, with strips of beading nailed to the inside, between which beading the sashes fit, and if the window is to be practicable, weights can be hung from sash-cords over pulleys in the orthodox way. A simpler non-practicable sash-window is suggested in Fig. 187.

In the long window (Fig. 231) the bars are of 1 in. square timber, halve-jointed. The bottom is canvassed. The curved bar at the top of the window suggested in the version on

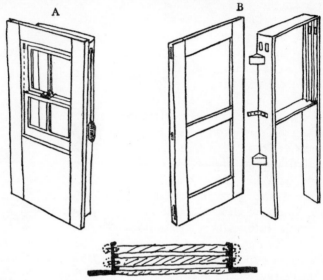

Fig. 230. Details of sash window construction.

Fig. 213 would be cut out of ply and nailed on the other bars.

In the cottage bay window (Fig. 232), the sides are hinged and the window-seat is slotted into place with loose-pin hinges; the ceiling of the bay is also hinged to work like a door-top reveal. The panes are suggested by crossed tapes, shown here partly complete. See also Fig. 187.

The fireplace framework (Fig. 233) is made of 6 in. × 1 in. floor board, faced with ply (the arch is in bent ply), and the hearth-projection is hinged to fold up for packing. The back view (Fig. 234) shows the backing and a fire flood, with, above the flood, several lengths of canvas attached to a handle, like a cat-o'-nine-tails, to waggle in front of the flood if the fire must appear to flicker. Another type of mantelpiece is shown in Fig. 187.

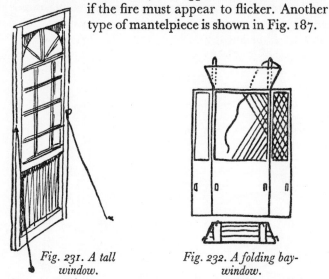

Fig. 231. A tall window.

Fig. 232. A folding bay-window.

The sideboard (Fig. 235) is perfectly straightforward, built in two parts so that either may be used separately on occasion.

Fig. 233. A simple fireplace.

Fig. 234. A fireplace from behind showing fire-flood and flicker effect.

The frames of the doors on·the top half are left unfilled to represent glazed doors, those of the bottom are ply-covered.

Lastly, the final scene in the theatre box we might develop to some decorative elaboration, but, reduced to its simplest, our requirements would be for a hinged groundrow to stand beyond our double doors with the sky cloth used behind as a backing and lit perhaps red. Fig. 236 shows the whole

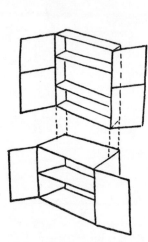

Fig. 235. A general-purpose cupboard.

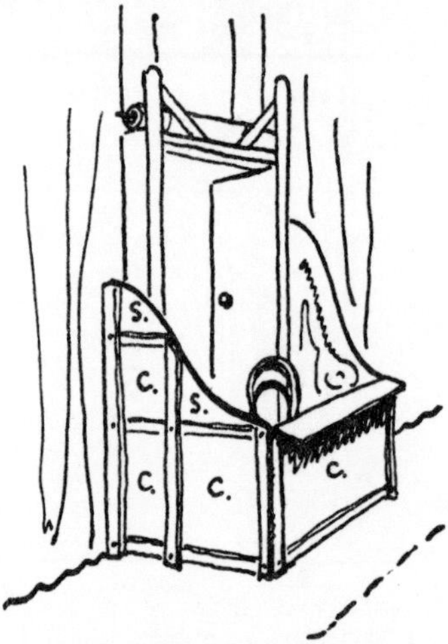

Fig. 236. The theatre-box in 'Abraham Lincoln' seen from behind.

viewed from the back with the position of the backing cloth shown by a dotted line. The box row consists of a back and two sides, the latter made of battened-out canvas (C) with the profile stiffened (S) by glued paper or ply. The back piece is provided with a red-plush-covered thickness piece at the top. This view shows the back of the double doors with the curtain-roll resting on the upper reveal.

Details and Script, 4: Three Specific Shows—2, *The Green Goddess*—Plotting and Arranging—Construction of Set-pieces, Arch-pieces, Rostrums and Steps

We have now the beginning of a scene-store, and our set of curtains, and we have had one instance of how to fit that set to a specific show, and how to make and arrange certain details belonging to the type I have called Representational Built Detail—that is, doors and windows and so forth, simple things that do not require a great deal of painting. Now we have to come again to our main issue: given the technicalities what is the art of making a show? How do we use all these elements in combination to make a piece of theatre? How do we make a show with them?

In practice the varieties of usage and arrangement are endless, but it will be useful to add to the detailed methods used in *Abraham Lincoln*, those which might be used for the setting of two other very frequently presented types of play, the straight modern drama and the Shakespearean play.

As an example of a straight modern drama, I shall take one that was written some years ago, but has proved popular, and is useful for my purpose in that it presents a range of three scenes widely different in nature, and contains one or two quite stiff problems. The whole approach to the setting of the show is typical of many other such dramas. The play is William Archer's *The Green Goddess*.

Let us picture a developing company of players whose progress has just brought them to the verge of Detail Setting. They have lately added to their resources a small hall, with very little head-room above the stage, but with a fixed proscenium in front of it. Their immediate demand in designing is still for economy. They possess a set of curtains (sides, back and border) made on the lines I have described and they hang them on a square of lashed battens, suspended from four pulleys above.

Their scenery-store is still small; they possess two single doors, and one double door, well-made in the way that we have discussed, and they know how to brace them in position. They have the sideboard-cupboard in two parts, upper and lower, which was made for *Abraham Lincoln*. And their small store of windows is there to be called upon, though it is of little use for the problem on hand.

Beyond this, they have nothing but a cash balance of, let us say, some four pounds for expenditure on scenery.

And before them lies *The Green Goddess*.

Let us look at the list of scenes. It contains one exterior and four interiors, pretty typical requirements, and the lines on which the problems are tackled will be useful knowledge for very many other plays.

The first scene is in the Himalayan mountains, by the shrine of the Green Goddess—a somewhat forbidding problem at first sight. And the last scene is inside the Green Goddess's temple, before the throne of her Chief Priest. These are two elaborate and important scenes, and if we are to get the character of the play and the local colour of India, we must succeed in these two scenes, whatever happens to the others. The second, third and fourth scenes of the play take place in two rooms of a Rajah's palace, furnished in Western style. Which means they are chamber-interiors offering much less chance for Indian atmosphere.

Now in the particular circumstance in which this play is produced we will suppose we are forced to watch for any opportunity of duplicating a setting or sparing ourselves the expense of creating a new one when an old one will do. These three scenes are in two rooms, a drawing-room, a small room with a wireless transmitting set in it, and the drawing-room again, and they are all in one act. It will be with some regret that our young company contemplates the problem of two scene-waits in one act, merely to take the action from one room to another and back again. And in such circumstances the question always arises: 'Granted the value of a change of scenery for the wireless-room and a change back after it, in a full-size theatre with adequate working conditions, is its value so very great in the limited conditions in which we are working? Or could we play all three scenes in one set without detriment to the action of the play?'

It has always to be taken into account that the playwright was working with other conditions than ours in mind, and may have introduced the change of scene in the middle of the act just for a break and a legitimate thrill of variety, and because in a full theatre his resources would allow it. If our resources do not allow it, we cannot afford that break.

If it introduced us to this problem alone, the consideration of this play would be worth while. You may often have to take similar liberties, and one of the arts of showmanship is to adapt the script to your working conditions.

We can manage the Himalayan shrine, and we can manage the temple of the Goddess, and we can furnish one rearrangement of our curtains for a normal interior, but whether because we have now used all our available material, or because we have already incurred two heavy scene-changes and cannot consider two more in the course of an act, we find our resources are at an end with the one interior set.

Now let us see what we can do. Imagine our grey curtain set (grey will suit both mountain rocks and a dim temple interior as well as an eastern room) arranged on our usual frame of battens, this time on the simple formula of a large central opening, three strips wide, in the back wall which we adopt because, firstly, our interior scenes demand a balcony overlooking a landscape, secondly, because our first scene demands a fair expanse of sky to represent an exterior, and that expanse of sky will be better displayed at the back than the side.

But we cannot have our opening dead centre, because we have also to accommodate in the back wall of the set the shrine and figure of the Green Goddess, according to the plot of the opening scene.

Why must this figure be placed at the back? Because of the way it must be made. And how is it to be made?

The Goddess will be a flat, cut-out, set-piece of ply-wood (braced behind with stiffening battens), or if the fire-authorities have influence over our presentation, the figure must be cut out of Oxylene, which is exactly like ply-wood except that it is fireproof (and costs more), or if we do decide to use ordinary ply-wood, we must, to comply with the regulations, canvas it on both sides before painting.

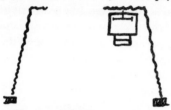

Fig. 237. 'The Green Goddess', first step.

Two alternative constructions are to make a proper set-piece with the orthodox open framing, profiling and canvassing in the fairly elaborate method of full-scenery technique, or to use the method of rough battening-out, with the brown-paper stiffening at the edges that we described earlier on p. 183. Whatever method we choose we have what is technically a painted set-piece, about four feet high, on which is a brightly coloured figure, many-armed and cross-legged.

We can set her on a small rostrum, say a couple of feet high and three feet square, to show her up the better, and in front of the rostrum we can place a short flight of two steps. As the figure is flat, it must face the audience, we cannot clearly have it at the side of the stage, showing in profile, because it has no profile to show. So it must go in the back wall.

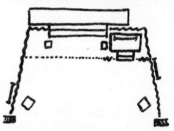

Fig. 238. 'The Green Goddess', plan of Act I.

Our talk with the producer has decided us that a large centre opening is necessary in the back wall, but to accommodate both opening and goddess-on-rostrum in the back wall of a small set, we must have the opening out of centre.

That then decides the rough shape of our beginnings and from it we get this arrangement (Fig. 237).

Our talk with the producer and our scene-plot further demand that the interior scene which is to follow must have a balcony overlooking a precipice, for over the balcony the butler who sends a false wireless message is thrown.

The only way to represent this is to have a rostrum at the back of the stage with a balustrade at its farther edge. And the rostrum must be high enough for a man to be dropped over, and crawl to the wings unseen, that is to say about two feet high. And yet the balustrade (which ought to be solid and not pierced) must be as low as possible so that the poor actor's drop from the hands of his murderers to the stage shall not be too great. Let us say three feet on top of the rostrum's height.

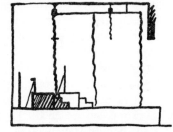

Fig. 239. 'The Green Goddess', section of Act I.

Now the striking and setting of a rostrum long enough not only to span the wide centre opening but to mask-in at the sides of the opening, is a difficult job. And it would be well to avoid moving it. Because of this, therefore, as well as for other, lesser reasons, we must try to use this rostrum as a standing feature of each scene, so that it stays in place throughout the play.

Fig. 240. 'The Green Goddess', setting of Act I.

The fitting of this rostrum then is the next move in our plan, and in Figs. 238 and 239 it is suggested with a long two-tread set of steps in front of it, cut, we may easily ask our audience to believe, out of the same rock in the mountain scene as the steps up to the shrine. And we intend to leave the rostrum set through the whole play.

But we have as yet made no indication of a shrine. There must be some suggestion that the figure of the goddess is housed here permanently and that the place is sacred.

A very simple way is to use two of our narrow curtains to

represent columns, supporting, we will imagine, a roof over the shrine. This use of narrow curtains as columns is often of great help. They are suspended from rings running on a strained wire (stretched across the framework of the set before it is pulled up) behind the border, or the second border, if two are used. Being on rings, we can move our curtain strips to wherever we want our pillars.

The furniture of the scene is simply four boxes placed where needed and standing for stones, a convention which, like the steps at the back, the audience accepts without any question (Fig. 240).

There is one other point about the plan for Act 1. We know that the next scene is to be an interior and, as we want to save all the time we can on the change, we brace our doors ready in place behind the curtains (Fig. 238). Then, in the change, all we must do is roll and pin the curtains in front, and they are disclosed ready in place to take their part in the scene. The entrances in the first scene are all from the rostrum in the centre-back opening, so we need no other way in. The backing for this opening is either a plain sky-cloth or, a backcloth with a simple arrangement of mountains painted on it, or, best of all, a cyclorama and a groundrow.

Now for the next act. The difficulty about Act II is that in the script it is divided into three scenes, firstly the drawing-room in the rajah's palace, secondly, a small room where a wireless transmitting set is housed behind locked doors, and thirdly the drawing-room once more. And we have decided that we cannot afford these two waits in one act, nor have we the material to build a second interior set. We get over the difficulties in the following way, and this is an example of the shifts to which a designer may be put in his day's work.

We house the wireless apparatus in a cupboard—the one from *Abraham Lincoln*—whose doors can be locked and we hide the cupboard, as is suggested in Figs. 241 and 242, behind a high, four-fold screen (shown in plan), which we may paint with an Indian design to give a colour-spot and a character to the scene, and we so arrange the screen that a man can stealthily open the left-hand door and creep directly behind the screen without the knowledge of persons in the room.

We can now produce every dramatic effect that a change of scene would have allowed, and this arrangement, with a little, but by no means unwelcome, stretch of the faith of the audience, and a very slight rearrangement of the script, saves us twenty minutes in the run of the play, the expense of another suite of furniture and a great deal of hurried energy.

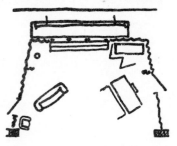

For the rest of the set, the two doors already in place are uncovered by rolling the curtains, and then we have to ask, how we are to fit the great space of sky outside the centre-back opening into an interior scheme. If a triple arch-piece is braced before the rostrum, in the opening,

Fig. 241. 'The Green Goddess', plan of Act II.

it will fill it, serve the exigencies of the play and give a note of oriental architecture. It is a very useful detail of scenery whose construction we will discuss later. The wireless cupboard is set where the shrine stood and the columns are cleared away to either side of the room. A carpet is laid cen-

Fig. 242. 'The Green Goddess', setting of Act II.

tre, and the furniture is set, among which I will ask you to keep in mind an arm-chair and a knee-hole pedestal desk. They come in handy, later, for the interior of the temple. A standard lamp is set in the corner, whose presence is demanded by the script, for the scene takes place in the evening and should have some source of illumination; and finally the balustrade is braced on the far edge of the rostrum. The view outside the window is the same as the back-scene of Act I. In Fig. 242 the furniture is shown only in plan.

Now we can run smoothly through Act II and come to the change for Act III.

Act III is the temple of the Green Goddess, with the high priest's throne, and we must make it without using a single element we have not used already. Save two large and brightly coloured shawls.

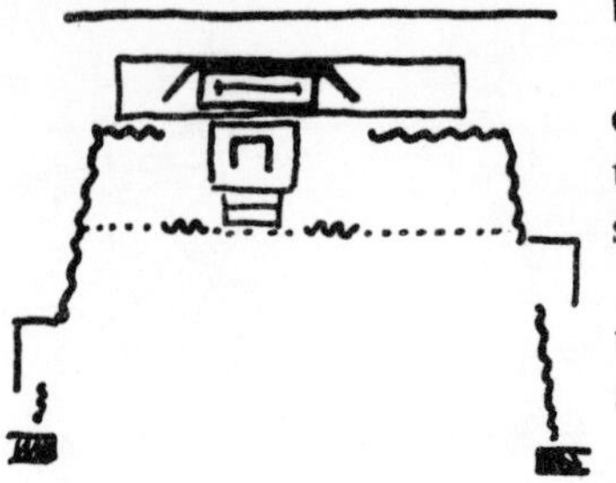

To begin with, we strike the doors (Fig. 243), leaving only the openings and their black screen-backings.

We also strike the long steps to the back rostrum, and the arches.

In front of this rostrum we now stand the small square rostrum from the first act, with its steps. On this we place the armchair and cover the whole with one of the large shawls, draping it with care and speed.

Fig. 243. 'The Green Goddess', plan of Act III.

Behind this, on the large rostrum, we stand the knee-hole desk and cover that with the other shawl, and then we stand the Goddess on the desk.

We cannot afford a second backcloth, so we have to take out all the lights on the original mountain-landscape and leave it dark, and, to help us, we may stand the screen from Act II behind the Goddess, presenting now the reverse face of the screen to the audience.

Fig. 244. 'The Green Goddess', setting of Act III.

Finally we add a note to the temple by pulling on our two 'columns' to stand either side the steps at the foot of the throne. And if we place them cunningly the audience will never realize that the throne is out of centre, though in Fig. 244 a suggestion is made of how the throne can be centralized, if there is time, by dropping the stage-right of the three rolled curtains of the back opening (see dotted lines).

If we now light our scene mostly from the footlights, we shall have done all we can to create the eerie atmosphere of the Temple of the Green Goddess.

And now a very brief note before we leave 'The Green Goddess' on the constructional side of such extra details as we need to add to our growing store. The new items are, the triple arch-piece, the set-piece of the goddess, the balustrade, the rostrums and the steps.

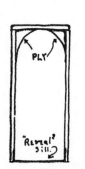

Fig. 245. The construction of a simple arch.

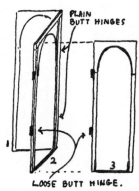

Fig. 246. The hingeing of three arch-pieces.

The construction of the arch-piece is very simple, and is shown in Fig. 245. Each of the three unit arches consists of two sides and a top of 3 in. × 1 in. mortise-and-tenon-jointed at the top corners, and supplied with a sill-iron at the bottom. The arch form is simply made by nailing two squares of ply, from each of which a quarter of a circle has been cut away, across the top corners of the frame, immediately strengthening the corner and obviating the need for cross-bracing.

Two of the arches are hinged together so as to fold face to face, the third is attached by means of a loose-butt hinge, and can be separated at will (Fig. 246). So, units of one single arch, a double arch, or a triple arch, are at the disposal of the designer, and he may use the full trio either flat, or in a three-sided bay, as in Fig. 247.

A very useful convention for a staircase in curtain-detail interiors is to set one arch in the side curtains with a three-tread set of steps going off through it.

The set-piece of the goddess we have discussed above. The balustrade-piece is similarly made by painting a three-foot wide strip of canvas as long as is needed to mask behind our opening, and nailing a 3 in. × 1 in. batten at the back to the top and the bottom. Across these, three short battens, one at either end and one in the centre, are nailed to stretch the top and bottom battens apart and the whole is ready to brace in place at the upstage edge of the rostrum. (Should we wish to cut out an arrangement of balusters in the canvas, we must

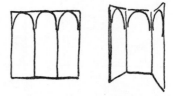

Fig. 247. The triple-arch piece in use.

either choose a fairly heavy close-weave hessian and give it a couple of coats of strong size before we paint it with fairly thick paint, then upon cutting out the intervals between the balusters with scissors the remaining stuff will stay reasonably stiff and flat, once it is battened out, to last a few performances. Or, and this is a better job, we use a lighter canvas and paint in normal thickness but, after cutting out, we must glue a thin black net, like a butter-muslin, behind the piece to re-inforce it and prevent the strips from curling. It is then battened-out as usual.) Full stage procedure would make an even better job but involves some knowledge of carpentry and jointing.

Lastly we must outline briefly the construction of stage rostrums. This is left to the last because it is perhaps the least simple piece of construction we shall treat in this book of simple setting and it too belongs rightly to full stage procedure, but some indication must be given here of the elements in order to make our survey reasonably complete.

Upon no other piece of apparatus in this book—unless it be the hanging-pulleys above—is the life of an actor likely to depend. But the first requirement of a rostrum is that it be firm. The second is that it be light, and the third that it should fold or else its bulk makes storing a problem. And so despite the urgent requirement that a rostrum be firm, we cannot build it solid—especially when it is of such a size as that at the back of the Green Goddess set. Here the dimensions may well be 3 ft. wide, 18 in. high and 14 ft. long. Even built as lightly as is consistent with strength, such a piece would be quite inconveniently difficult to shift in one. It must therefore be in sections, and not only in sections, but, to make it possible to store, folding sections.

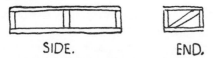

SIDE.   END.

Fig. 248. Front and side elevations of rostrum base.

We may divide it into either two or three. Two 7 ft. sections would be more convenient provided we have stage-hands capable of shifting a 7 ft. rostrum top—which is not light. If we have not we must make two 5 ft. sections and one 4 ft. Let us discuss the construction of one of these sections, the others, and that upon which the goddess is set, will be exactly similar.

A stage rostrum consists of four sides and a top. The sides are each built similarly and consist of a frame of 3 in. × 1 in. with a centre rail—exactly like a smaller version of one leaf of our first simple screen, but standing now of course upon its side (Fig. 248). The ends are similar, but, in a 3 ft. wide rostrum, need not necessarily have a centre rail, though a cross-brace to keep them square is useful. In these frames, of course, no butt-jointing can be allowed (save on the cross-brace), all joints should be true and well-fitting mortise-and-tenons. Next, the two sides and the two ends are assembled and hinged together. The principle of hingeing should be observed with some care. The ends are to be nested inside the sides so that they stand in flush with the ends of the sides (Fig. 249). Two hinges are used at each corner, one at the top and one at the bottom. At two opposite corners the hinges are attached normally to the inside, at the other two opposite corners the hinges are put on in a different way. Look at Fig. 249, the hinges A and B are straightforwardly applied and need not be inset. But at C and D one flap of the hinge is inset

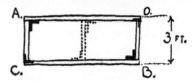

Fig. 249. Plan of rostrum base.

and screwed to the inner side of the side, the other, inset and screwed to the outer side of the end. Now the whole base will fold up through Fig. 250 and pack quite flat as in Fig. 251. Any rostrum over 4 ft. long should have a centre frame, exactly similar to the end, hinged across the middle as the dotted lines in Fig. 249 show.

The top is simple. It consists of 1 in. floor-boards battened together below with lengths of 3 in. × 1 in. The main point to

Fig. 250. Rostrum base   *Fig. 251. Rostrum base*
part-folded.   *fully folded.*

notice is that the battens are set in from the ends of the boards, and also cut short at their own ends, by a distance equal to the thickness of the wood of the frames, so that when the base is opened and the top laid upon it, the battens fit *inside* the base-top and the underside of the top-boards lies directly on the top edge of the base-frames. If the rostrum is long and has a centre frame then two battens are added on the underside of the top as indicated by dotted lines in Fig. 252, and these drop either side of the centre frame.

To conclude, the two-tread set of steps to approach such a rostrum is a fairly straightforward job (Fig. 253). It is made almost entirely of 6 in. and 9 in. floor-boards, 1 in. thick. The standard dimension of stage steps is 6 in. risers and 9 in.

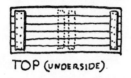

TOP (UNDERSIDE).

Fig. 252. Plan of rostrum top.

treads. The front edge of each tread should be laid on the top edge of the riser below. The supports are the two end-pieces and, if the steps are wider then 3 ft., a centre piece. These are composed of a 17 in. piece of 6 in. board and an 8 in. piece

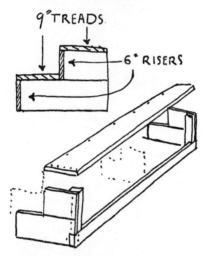

9″ TREADS.

6″ RISERS

Fig. 253. Simple 2-tread set of steps.

above it, as in the diagram, battened-out behind by one piece of 3 in. × 1 in. To the edges of this the steps are securely nailed. It makes for rigidity if a batten of 3 in. × 1 in. is let in and nailed across the bottom of the back.

In setting the three elements, rostrum, arch-piece and steps, on the stage, it will be found, when the arch is braced in place on the stage in front of the rostrum, that the thickness of the arch-battens will cause a gap at the threshold of each opening between rostrum and step (Fig. 254). To fill this, three strips

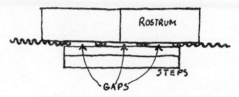

Fig. 254. A difficulty to be watched in the setting of the steps.

of 1 in. square wood should be nailed for the occasion to the back edge of the top tread so as to fit in the archways. Further, as the rostrum itself forms the third step up, it follows that a riser must be provided between the top step and the rostrum-top itself. This filling-piece is simply a 6 in. wide strip of ply nailed across the top part of that side of the rostrum base.

Details and Script, 5: Three Specific Shows—
3, *Romeo and Juliet*

Let us turn now to the Shakespeare play. We will choose one with a variety of scenes, one with examples of a public square, a great hall, a balcony scene, a cell, and a tomb—and *Romeo and Juliet* comes at once to mind.

Before we tackle the actual details of arrangement for this play there are one or two very useful points to be noted that apply to all of its type.

The play may receive a good deal of blue-pencilling by the producer before it can be reduced to a length suitable for his purpose, especially with the modern, slow style of speaking verse, and I shall take a version used a few years ago, which contained exactly twenty scenes. Now such a play would be practically impossible to stage in these simple circumstances, if we have to drop the tabs, put up the house-lights, change our set, put out the house-lights, and raise our tabs between scenes. Obviously something quicker is needed. We must adopt the Traverse Curtain.

The construction of the play is in many scenes, some long and important, some short and slight. And these long and short scenes are interspersed with a planning that makes it broadly possible to set a big scene (for a long scene is always a big scene—that is one with several characters, requiring a large area) in a space behind a curtain at the back of the stage, while the preceding short scene, which contains perhaps only a couple of characters, is being played on the stage proper in front. Here we see the importance of the traverse whereby, at the conclusion of a large scene, we can draw a curtain across at the centre or towards the back of the stage, to provide the background for a simple front-stage scene. And as the actors enter to play their parts on the front-stage, the stage-hands run on behind this traverse curtain and strike the old scene and set the next large set.

In the script, however, the sandwiching of long and short scenes is not invariable; if it were, it would result in monotony and an uncomfortably close restriction on the playwright in unfolding his plot. Hence arises the modern theory of three stages. This system divides the stage proper into (*a*) 'fore-stage', corresponding very roughly with the Elizabethan apron-stage, that part projecting into the pit and possibly uncovered by the stage-roof, (*b*) the 'middle stage' corresponding with the whole of the Elizabethan platform, and (*c*) the 'upper stage' or deepest stage corresponding to the Eliza-

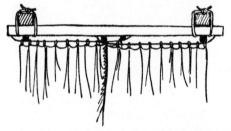

Fig. 255. A traverse batten slung under *the side battens.*

bethan 'inner' stage, which was an opening in the tiring-house, with a curtain closing it.

If we imagine a curtain set with one pair of traverse curtains a little way back from the proscenium, we can obviously rely on two acting-areas, one in front of the traverse, which will probably be small, where no furniture may be used unless it is set and struck in sight of the audience, or when the front tabs are closed, and a second, the size of the whole stage, where furniture and painted details may be altered so long as they are set above the traverse-line, so as to be changed during the run of a front scene. Further, if our resources (and our pulleys in the roof) will bear a second set of traverse curtains farther upstage, we can face almost any play with a very good chance of keeping up the interest all the way through, and avoiding a monotonous alternation.

This traverse is to the curtain set an addition that we have noted on p. 129. The traverse may be added at any depth of the stage, and more than one may be put in, provided each is run on its own battens and wires.

But we shall add a considerable weight on those four original pulleys that formed the simplest arrangement from which to hang our set. We must be very sure that they will stand it. Otherwise we must put in two more sets of pulleys and hang the traverses independently from them. Or else we can support the corners of our batten framework on special long upright braces.

The battens carrying the traverses must be lashed to the *under* side of the side battens if they are hung from the curtain-frame—so that the wires are left free (Fig. 255). Better to suspend each on its own set of lines.

Now as to our plan.

We make a list of the scenes and very carefully go through them with the script.

Scene 1. (I am going to number the scenes from one to twenty, instead of numbering them as in the script, from which we have to cut several small scenes entirely—I do not advocate such cutting, but am following the general fashion.) —Scene 1 contains a sword-fight between the partisans of the rival houses. For this a full stage is essential. That is our starting-point.

We begin by listing these twenty scenes, and then we have to add against each a note of that part of the stage on which it is most conveniently played; on the full stage, or before the upstage traverse, or before the downstage traverse. One or two other features are added to the list later.

I.   1. A Public Place.   Full stage.
    2. Capulet's House.   Traverse U.
    3. A Street.   Traverse D.
    4. Hall, Capulet's House.   Full stage.
    5. Near Capulet's Orchard. Traverse D.
    6. Capulet's Orchard.   Full stage. Balcony left.
    7. Friar Lawrence's Cell.   Traverse D, gates.
    8. A Public Place.   Full stage.

	9. Capulet's House.	Traverse U.
	10. Friar Lawrence's Cell.	Traverse D, gates.
	11. A Public Place.	Full stage.
II.	12. Capulet's House.	Traverse U.
	13. Friar Lawrence's Cell.	Traverse D, gates.
	14. In Capulet's House.	Traverse U.
	15. Juliet's Bedchamber.	Full stage.
	16. Friar Lawrence's Cell.	Traverse D, gates.
	17. Bedchamber.	Full stage.
III.	18. Mantua.	Traverse D.
	19. Friar Lawrence's Cell.	Traverse D.
	20. Tomb.	Full stage.

Now glancing through the script, we find that Scene 4, the party in Capulet's house, must have a clear stage for a dance and a fair number of people. We note this on the above list.

To Scene 6, the famous balcony scene, we will give a full stage, just for old times' sake.

Scene 8, A public place, needs a number of people and a full stage as does Scene 11.

We can play now in small sets until Scene 15, the Bedroom Scene, where we need a full set once more, chiefly because of the space the bed takes up and the fact that we need a window, which we can best place in the back wall of the set. And Scene 17 is the same.

Lastly, for the Tomb Scene, which concludes, in which many people again meet, and in which we have to set the bier itself, we need the full stage.

Now we have an arrangement carefully thought out to allow of every full-stage scene being set while a preceding short scene is played before one or other of the traverse curtains.

The next question is 'intervals'.

Intervals must come both where the play gives psychological opportunity and where they may be of most use to the scene-shifters.

The two difficult scenes to arrange in the latter half of the play are the tomb scene and the bedroom scene. The tomb scene is preceded by two short scenes and then the bedroom, so we have to strike the bedroom and set the tomb in the space of two very short front scenes, which is a biggish change. We find we can logically have a break before the first of those two short scenes, Scene 18, so let us put the second interval here.

Next we have to ask ourselves at what point we can begin setting the bedroom.

Let us notice where the last Public-Square scene comes. It is Scene 11. After that we need our full stage only for the bedroom and the tomb. So let us set the bedroom after Scene 11 and during the succeeding short scenes, giving ourselves a good start by putting the first interval between Scenes 11 and 12.

Now to sort out the traverse scenes. The first two are Scenes 2 and 3, of which Scene 2 has more people, so let us make that the large or upstage traverse scene, and Scene 3 the shallow traverse. The upstage and the downstage traverses we will label respectively U and D.

Scene 5 is probably a street, so we use what we used last time for a street—Traverse D. Our second reason for using the downstage traverse here, is that we need as much space as possible behind for setting the balcony scene.

A further interesting point enters here. Sometimes it is possible to leave a character upon the stage at the end of a forestage scene and, turning him with his back to the audience, open the traverse and send the player striding upstage forthwith immediately into the succeeding scene. Such a transition is useful here. Let us set Scene 5 in a street outside the Orchard. We find Romeo's friends leaving him to climb the wall and seek the balcony. As they go off, we may open the traverse and the Garden to Romeo and he may walk straight into the Garden instead of popping off till the traverse opens and popping on again immediately it is clear.

For Scene 7, as we have to cover the stage again in order to strike the balcony, we must again use the downstage traverse.

Scene 9 is as Scene 2. And as there is no furniture in the public square scene to clear away we can conceal the whole set with the upstage traverse. And we can draw traverse D over that again for the Scene 10, opening both for Scene 11.

Now comes the interval in which we can set our bedroom scene at the back of the stage, and conceal it for the first three scenes of the act with the traverses, using as before the upstage for Capulet's house, and the downstage for the cell, and we then draw the downstage traverse across for the cell again in Scene 16, after the first bedroom scene. After the second bedroom scene (Scene 17) comes the second interval.

Now in the act-wait we can strike the bedroom, set the

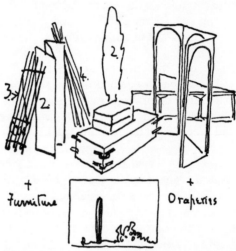

Fig. 256. The scenery-store for the twenty scenes of 'Romeo and Juliet'.

tomb, and play Scene 18 before traverse D, with a slight variance, perhaps only a change of light for Scene 19, and then open traverse D finally to disclose the full tomb scene.

There in a few words is summarily described a scheme that in itself took a day and a half to work out in closest touch with the producer.

Next, how did we make the scenery, and what did the scenes look like?

Fig. 256 shows us our complete scene-store for *Romeo and Juliet*. To the left of the group is a property iron gate, made of dowel-rods and ply circles, three of these gates were made.

Next is a three-fold screen of which we need a pair.

Leaning against that are four poles with which we make the bedposts.

In the centre at the back is one of a pair of profiled cypress trees, and in front a 6 ft. × 2 ft. 6 in. rostrum, 2 ft. high, and upon it two boxes, 3 ft. × 2 ft. × 9 in. To the corners of the rostrum are fixed metal straps to take the bed-posts.

To the right is our old friend the triple-arch, and behind it a groundrow balustrade, hinged in the centre if necessary for transport.

Fig. 257. 'Romeo and Juliet.' A Public Square.

Below is noted the addition of certain pieces of furniture and, of course, of the curtain set itself, and such other draperies as window curtains.

In the centre is shown the optional detail of a very simple painted backcloth, consisting of a perfectly plain, pale sky, with a strip of plain bright green at the bottom, carefully painted as to its upper edge to give the texture of grass, and extending up at the left into a small cypress, shadowed with black, with perhaps a dull brown trunk, and at the right into a rose bush similarly shadowed, and with large white wild roses here and there. The size and scale of such a cloth are not suggested in the figure as they must depend always upon the size of the set and the stage.

Fig. 258. 'Romeo and Juliet.' The Friar's Cell.

In Fig. 257 is the plan and the general appearance of the Open Square scene. In Fig. 258 is the Friar's Cell, made with the downstage traverse partly closed and a gate stood in the

Fig. 259. 'Romeo and Juliet.' In Capulet's House.

gap. The gate is never opened in the cell scenes, and the upstage traverse is closed to form a backing.

Fig. 259 shows a room in Capulet's house, set simply by two screens (their leaves perhaps painted with heraldic de-

240

vices) in front of the upstage traverse. The plan notes the
position of a table and a chair, the only furniture.

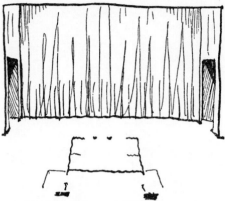

Fig. 260. 'Romeo and Juliet.' A street.

Fig. 260 is completely plain, the downstage traverse, for the
street scenes.

Fig. 261 is the Banquet Hall with the two outer arches

Fig. 261. 'Romeo and Juliet.' Capulet's Ballroom.

backed by the screens (now showing the reverse side) leaving
the centre arch to open on a suggestion of a small balcony.

The Balcony Scene (Fig. 262), is given a variation in shape
by bringing both sets of traverse curtains slightly on, which

also moves the balcony more to the centre of the stage, so that even in theatres with difficult sight-lines all the audience

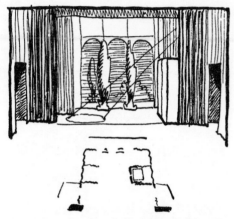

Fig. 262. 'Romeo and Juliet.' The Balcony Scene.

will be able to see Juliet. The balcony itself consists of the rostrum with the two boxes on top of it (giving a floor 3 ft. 6 in. high) and the whole masked by the screens again showing the

Fig. 263. 'Romeo and Juliet.' The Bedroom Scene.

plain reverse side. The pillars of the arches are masked by the two trees. The light is dim and chiefly from a spot behind Juliet.

Fig. 263 shows the Bedroom. Here the rostrum is provided with its posts and about the tops of these a valance is hung, the bed is made and a valance is hung round the rostrum; a curtain on a rod is hung across the window. The window is represented simply by moving the balustrade at the back close to the arches. Upon the balustrade, the hooks of a rope-ladder are hung.

Fig. 264. 'Romeo and Juliet.' The Tomb Scene.

And the last scene (Fig. 264) the Tomb, is made by fitting the three gates in the three arches and hanging torch-extinguishers from the springs of the arches where a decorative capital had been painted for the other scenes. Juliet lies right of centre upon the rostrum raised on the two boxes. The centre gate can be opened.

And that is all.

SECTION 25

A Simple Special Arrangement

Before leaving the subject of the Detail Setting a very useful and practical formula calls for inclusion. It is suitable to almost any scene where more or less realistic-type interiors are played in curtains in a largish theatre.

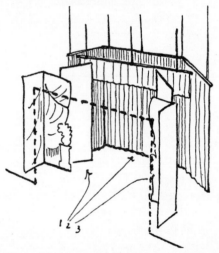

Fig. 265. A useful curtain formula for festivals in large theatres.

It is an interesting variant of the 'Frame' detail setting combined with a 'representational built detail' group in the centre of the back curtains.

It is shown in Figs. 265 and 266. In Fig. 265 the proscenium proper is represented as transparent. Behind it is a pair of booked proscenium wings, behind these again are two black wings, labelled 1 and 3, with a black velvet border just behind

244

and above. Finally the background consists of an armed batten hung with black velvet curtains, in the centre lower part
of which a space can be cleared either by rolling up strips, or
by draping. This space is labelled 2.

Now parts 1, 2 and 3 are the only parts of the set where
changeable scenery has to be considered. All settings are arranged to contain their moveable scenery-details either
downstage right or left, or upstage centre.

The flats 1 and 3 may have fireplaces set before them, may

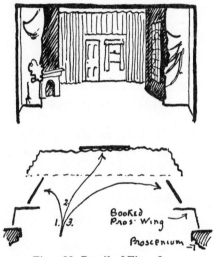

Fig. 266. Detail of Fig. 265.

be left plain, may be hung with a determinating detail (picture, mirror and the like) or may be exchanged for door or
window flats, the plain part of the flat being still black. These
openings must, of course, be provided with backings. Further, against the plain flats we may stand some essential piece
of furniture such as a sideboard or a throne. Before these
'firm walls' furniture or properties can be grouped, and they
supply an area of flatness often so much needed in a curtain
set.

So useful can these plain 'background' spaces be in practice that the designs of different sets may compete with each
other to see which shall most significantly utilize the plain

spaces 1 and 2 as backings to set off a most carefully chosen object that shall stamp the scene. And one of the first questions the designer asks himself is 'Now what exactly can we find most effective to put against—or how most effectively can we use—the two plain side wings this time?'

Similarly in the part labelled 2, changes can be made. Either the space can be left plain, that is, the curtains may hang undisturbed, or a background screen can be stood in front of the curtains. If it contain a door or window, the curtains behind may be draped aside to allow a backing beyond to show, or the screen may be within the curtains and the curtain widths in front of the piece rolled up to reveal it and pinned just as in Section 19. Such a piece as that shown in Fig. 42 is very suitable here. And the principle governing it— namely the concentration of the whole nature of a room into a small group of essentials at the back—is just as useful a guide.

Another method is to hang the back curtains on runners so that they form a traverse which can be part-opened, then the opening may be filled with a full-sized flat or a group of flats specially painted in accordance with the concentration-of-essentials principle mentioned above.

This central piece (2 in Fig. 265) and its backings offer the only surface that may, generally speaking, be painted—of course if windows are used in flats 1 and 2 painted backings to these may be made. By 'painted' I do not simply mean 'coloured', for, of course, any made detail must be coloured, but painted with some representative design or pattern expressive of the scene to be played.

The designer is offered a well-defined and interesting problem, every time he sets a scene, of deciding how, when he has disposed of his side wings, and so fixed the details of his *frame*, he may turn to the centre of his composition and in its small area say just as much as he wants about what I might call the 'pictorial' side of his set, untroubled about the extension of that pictorial note to cover the whole area of the set. That extension, he will find, is his problem in full scenery.

Properly understood and used, this formula of setting is most suitable for shows consisting of several scenes, where conditions forbid a full scene-change each time—shows, for instance, such as bills of one-act plays, festivals, reviews o. variety concerts and groups of sketches.

An extremely important variant of the Detail Setting is growing up to-day in which the stage-setting consists of sides (made of curtains, flats or frame details) with a back in the form of a cyclorama or stage sky. In such a surround are set details of the variety we have discussed. But then at length our style steps clear of the Detail Setting and reaches the further category of Cyclorama Setting.

The most modern account perhaps would discuss Detail Setting and Cyclorama Setting under one head as 'details of scenery set against a non-determined background *or* sky', but such a wide definition would take us too far from the field of simpler settings and lead us into some of the more advanced forms of full theatre technique, until we reached at length the problem of the Ninth Variety of Detail Setting, namely *The Projected Detail*, where no actual scenery is used at all and only an image is thrown upon the back wall from a lantern. This it seems inexpedient to do before examining at length that other wide field which as yet we have not touched— the Technique of Standard Full-theatre Setting and Scenery.

SECTION 26

Finale—Standardization and Specification

Let us now look into the future for a moment, not like a visionary, but with purely practical intent.

Certain organizations have of late done much to increase the amateur movement, and one result has been the growth of a visiting system in which—whether upon the occasion of a theatre festival or for another reason—companies of players come from a distance and present shows upon a strange stage.

Such 'touring' is an ancient feature of the theatre, but it brings into still greater prominence the subject of setting the show. How are the travellers to set their scenes? What are they to bring, what borrow, and what expect to find in the host-theatre? In the past the strolling players evolved various techniques designed to reduce the scenery without spoiling the show as a show. To-day the amateurs—by whom acting is sometimes held in far too high regard as a sole end—seek also to reduce the scenery for their festivals, *but quite forget in doing so to avoid spoiling the show*. The result is that modern festival settings are among the poorest makeshifts in the amateur programme. And an annual festival at a big centre should surely be the occasion for some of the most interesting work of the year in that department and *consistent with festival conditions*.

In the last phrase lies the whole problem and the whole weakness, for the conditions are not good enough. We must outline an improvement.

Not only are the conditions not good enough but this is often fully realized and complacently accepted without a single step being taken to remedy the glaring inadequacy. So

248

often is the excuse made of the difficulty of the problem and so often are the adjudicators asked to overlook certain slovenlinesses for which the conditions are blamed that it sometimes comes to one to wonder whether there does not lie behind these apologies a serious idleness or ignorance in the organizers. . . .

Poverty is a plea we cannot allow them. Poverty may well make their progress difficult, but the straitest circumstances in the world cannot prevent a company drawing up on a sheet of notepaper a list of its essential needs and watching, watching all the time for an opportunity to snatch something to supply one or another of these, till, year by year, the items are one by one crossed off. Even should nothing ever turn up, I could forgive the company's hard case, but I cannot forgive the company that goes on with its bad material and bad conditions *without a plan of what it would have if it could get it.* That is idleness and ignorance.

Festival-organizer after festival-organizer has told me it is impossible to improve conditions. And festival-organizer after festival-organizer has told me upon my enquiry that, if he had the chance to make improvements, he has not the vaguest plan for beginning.

To such I wish to submit a practical suggestion in this last section. It will be a suggestion remarkable for its conservatism. It will give no plan for a complete new style of setting—developments I leave to the designers in the companies—it will take no step forward, it will merely recommend a setting-in-order of the existing conditions.

Let us attempt to set out how a stage *should* be equipped.

Could we but make what follows an accepted standard all over Great Britain, we should be able to rule that no theatre failing in respect of any of the following points should ever be allowed or invited to stand host to a visiting company, at any rate on so important an occasion as a festival of Theatre.

We can make the equipment of a stage the subject of a specification. This specification, once thought out and clearly drawn up is a guide not only to the visiting companies, helping them to realize beforehand exactly what conditions they may expect, but is a guide also to each theatre which opens its doors to visitors, showing what common courtesy and the interests of theatre require it to contribute to a show, and in what directions—supposing its equipment is incomplete—it must aim to develop when occasion allows.

Under what heads should a specification of equipment and resources be made and what should each head contain? Primarily, there must be four heads: The Curtains, The Details of Scenery, The Furniture, The Lighting. And what should be contained under each of these four?

THE CURTAINS. The Curtain Set should *always* be made of separate widths, and upon this anatomy the description of the set should be based. Just as we describe a locomotive under the symbol of say, 4—6—4, so may we describe a curtain set in convenient formula based on the symbol a—b—a, the first and the last factors representing the number of curtain-strips in the sides, and the centre factor, the number in the back. If now we send to a visiting company the code—'Curtains, silver-grey, 3–5–3', and standardize our curtain width as 3 ft., the company know a great deal about the set they have to play in.

Generally the back curtains should be capable of the usual rolled openings and *also* be on traverse lines so as to offer the alternative of drawing back to the sides to allow of a development in setting that we shall mention in a moment.

It should be the business of the theatre (and not the visiting company) to see that this set presents a neat appearance and *masks*. It may or may not be necessary to add to the above specification-code—'1 border' or '2 borders', but it should be the theatre's business to see that these borders are adequate for masking, are properly placed and are as few as possible.

In those rare cases where alternative colours are provided on the reverse of the curtains, this should also be specified.

Concerning this standard setting, another element should be just as regular and as much to be depended upon by visitors as the curtains themselves, that is an adequate sky-backing behind. Ideally this should be a cyclorama, but this is a factor still in its infancy and scarcely belongs to our subject of simple setting. A very wise and valuable step can be taken, however, in this direction; it should be the aim of every theatre to have its stage back-wall rendered flat and plastered over its whole extent to serve as a sky. If this is structurally or financially impossible—and even then the scheme should be kept in mind and eternally pressed for—*a properly painted and hung sky-cloth is absolutely essential.* Every visiting company should expect and demand it as part of every theatre's inevitable equipment. It will then be possible to extend the field of festival setting—at the moment too cripplingly limited by the rule that 'all teams must play in the curtains provided'—to include the new and infant style about which experiment would be so welcome, Cyclorama Setting. Any encouragement of such a movement is an advance. All festival rules should allow three alternatives: (*a*) Setting in curtains with built details, (*b*) Setting in curtains with painted details, (*c*) Setting with details against a Cyclorama.

Indispensable to the sky-cloth is its adequate lighting equipment. This we will discuss in its place.

THE DETAILS. Any hall opening its doors to visiting theatrical companies should regard as an obligation of its hospitality the provision of the following details of scenery to be lent when required. These should be kept in good repair, always neatly painted and *painted in a standard simple colour*, preferably a plain brown. These are special standard loan articles and no visitor should be allowed to alter them in any way or paint anything upon them, but should return them exactly as received. They are loan articles and standard articles and should be constructed and featured as such, and be the barest, simplest symbols, well-built but devoid of any particularization or decoration.

A company may use these or not as it choses. No attempt whatever should be made to force them upon a visitor, but if accepted they must be used exactly as they are (save perhaps for the pinning upon them of determinating sub-details such as special panels or labels upon the doors and so forth— details which can be removed afterwards without any damage to or defacing of the original piece). If a company desire any detail different either in shape or colour from the existing stock, it must supply and bring its own.

It is the view of certain people (among whom am I) that a company should always supply and work with its own details, but I am quite prepared to admit not only the possible difficulties and expenses of transport, but that very many modern plays do not actually demand to be 'set' at all—they merely need certain simple representational built details of doors, windows and fireplaces. For such plays, and for companies presenting them for their face value and not seeking to give a special note with the setting, it is pointless to supply special doors and the rest. They may just as well borrow. With the painted detail the case is completely different; the painted detail should always be supplied by the company. As also should the screw-eyes behind to take the braces. The braces themselves and their stage-screws or weights should be lent by the theatre.

Such a loan store of details need not be large but there is an irreducible minimum. Every stage offering its hospitality should be able to provide the following:

2 plain doors (with reversible pin-hinges to open any way).

1 double French window (perhaps with the windows interchangeable with plain leaves so as to give a double door).

1 simple sash or casement window.

1 simple fireplace.

2 double-leaf screen door-backings (painted standard grey or black).

1 double-leaf screen fireplace-backing.

3 18 in. high rostrums (say 3 ft. × 5 ft. each, these measurements, however, depend on the stage, the trio in a line should span the back of the set).

3 2-tread steps (each as long as a rostrum).

The visiting company must supply all painted details (with provision for support-attachments), all backings to side windows, any piece of a special colour, any piece of a special shape and anything not on the theatre's list.

THE FURNITURE. Similarly there is no need, in certain styles of presentation of certain plays, to bring the more ordinary articles of furniture; to a certain point the theatre may supply these. It should, however, very clearly mark a limit.

It is in the very highest degree undesirable that it should pamper idle companies by accepting a carelessly specified furniture-list, and exert much energy to collect odd pieces with no knowledge of the show and their suitability to it. That which a company may expect to find and that which it is expected to bring should be much more clearly specified and understood; then we should have less of that nonsense in which a company from fifty miles away keeps the busy resident stage-manager of its host theatre worrying for three days to find a sofa with one end and no back just because the author of their play about a cottage kitchen whimsically suggested there should be one by the window.

On the other hand there is no reason at all why some rational economy should not be exercised on account of those many, many kitchen-plays, or even of certain faintly determined drawing-room plays. For these (again when presented in a certain way) any suitable chair is as good as another and much the best way is to accept a convention and supply stock furniture. The extent of such a stock is indicated below. Every detail should be of a clear, simple shape and free from any particularizing feature—as plain and forthright and good as possible.

6 Windsor (wheel-back) chairs, four of which should be plain and two with arms. These should be darkish brown in colour (stained cleanly over the white wood with a non-varnish stain), and not polished but quite dull in surface. This type of chair is suitable at a pinch in any kitchen not specially particularized in type (otherwise the furniture must be supplied by the company) and is not unsuitable even if called upon for occasional chairs to supplement the furniture of a living-room. Further it is a fine English traditional shape.

1 plain kitchen table (firm, and stained like the chairs).

1 Chesterfield suite, as good, but as simple in line, as possible, comprising the usual upholstered settee and two armchairs. For these there may be provided a set, or a series of sets, of loose covers, plain and patterned. If there is only one set it should be a quiet, fairly strong, plain

colour—a dull wine-colour, a rich brown or a darkish strong green. Other sets of covers might be (*a*) bright chintz, (*b*) dull, middle-tone and dowdy.

2 simple occasional tables.

1 large table, most usefully in three sections and specially made to give either a normal ordinary-sized oblong table, two semi-circular tables (which together make a small round table), or altogether a long dining-table with rounded ends.

1 plain fireplace-hearth curb.

Window curtains for sash window and French windows, 1 set cream. 1 set to match (in type if not in pattern) each set of chair covers.

6 cushions with covers to match as above.

1 divan with covers to match as above.

These are the essentials, if the store were to grow its next steps might well be, in order of importance, a desk, a sideboard, a bookcase, a cupboard.

All further pieces to those listed above, all ornaments and all properties should be made, absolutely firmly, the affair of the companies. They should also be encouraged to bring their own hangings and covers.

Here I would, in passing, remind companies, as opposed to theatres, of the value of another and completely different type of furniture, home-designed and made in white wood, able to be painted or covered to suit many occasions, and pin-hinged for convenience in travelling. There is a wide field for the practical designer. The results may be very different from the stock stuff in effect, highly particularized and of the greatest value to the show as a whole.

LIGHTING. It is not my intention to discuss any technicalities. These have had full treatment by other pens. What follows is no attempt to limit lighting sets to one form throughout Great Britain, nor even to recommend an ideal equipment. It merely makes one suggestion to help the uninitiated to grasp the simplest aspect of an adequate lighting system that, for some reason, he persists in regarding as so incomprehensibly complicated. I make no unwise claim (as some do) that the understanding and installing of stage-circuits and wiring is anyone's job; it is not. Any more than scene-painting is. It also is a specialist's department. But concerning stage lighting equipments as a whole, every member of a theatre's company who is open to know anything about the stage at all should realize that a complete lighting system may be reduced to five essential lamps or rows of lamps.

It is as simple as that. There are two sources of light at the top, and one either side, and one in front. Let us examine this quintette.

1. The first source of light is a lamp, or better a row of lamps above, just behind the top of the proscenium opening. It is called the 'No. 1 Batten' or the 'Pross Batten' ('batten' is here an ellipsis for 'batten of lamps'). It should light the stage and actors, never the scenery.

2. The second source of light is a lamp, or far better a row of lamps, to light the back scenery, and is hung across upstage, a few feet in front of the back wall. It is called the 'Sky Batten' or 'Back Batten'. It should never light the stage or the actors, only the back scene.

3 and 4. The third and fourth sources of light are (generally) single lamps, one either side the stage in the wings, each on a standard and fed by a long flexible lead so as to be placed at any point in the wings. They are called 'Backing Floods' and may occasionally be taken off their stands and stood on the floor, upstage, at the foot of the backcloth to light it from below. The points to which these floods are connected are, on the full stage, under small trapdoors in the stage floor and are hence called 'Dips', occasionally the term is extended to cover in effect the side lamps themselves.

5. The fifth source of light is one or more lamps, each in a focussing- or spot-lantern, and situated in the auditorium. These are called the front-of-house spots or 'F.O.H. Spots'. They should light the actors and (generally speaking) never the scenery.

Having established the Five Fundamentals, we may make our single qualification; there is to be added sometimes (and far more often than some extremists admit) that very useful and traditional sixth source of light, from below and in front —the footlights or (an older name and though now not apt, still one that has stuck) the 'Floats'. These are very often useful and in one set of conditions at least—that is where there is no F.O.H. lighting—essential. They should be arranged so as not to strike the lower part of the back scene.

What developments and extensions of these five (or six) fundamentals are possible it is not in my territory to consider, but the reduction of what often seems a vast and complicated installation to no more than five units allows me to stress what are the points of first importance in the arrangement of lights, and to offer a convenient criterion by which to judge or describe the equipment of a theatre, and is sufficient for the purpose I have at the moment of drawing up a form of specification for theatres. An extension of this note on lighting is offered by the figures in the model specification on p. 259, for which I acknowledge Harold Ridge's kind help.

If now these elemental requirements of Stage-setting, Details, Furniture and Lighting be observed, we find ourselves in a much clearer and more possible position. Any intending visitors to a theatre have but to send a postcard saying: 'What are the specifications of your theatre?' and in return they would receive all the information they need. We might even go so far to simplify things as to supply each host-theatre with the following form, copies of which duly filled in would most usefully describe the current conditions, so far as concerns setting, at that theatre (see Fig. 267).

This specification of setting equipment might be labelled 'Document A' in the theatre's identity papers, but I do not want to give the impression that it alone represents anything like sufficiently what each theatre should set down in black and white about itself. Notice that it pretends to be nothing more than a specification of *setting equipment*. Always up to it in importance—and sometimes far more important—will be a paper we must here cryptically name 'Document B'. This must contain the *eight essential measurements* by which the theatre conveys the secrets of its sight-lines to a setting-designer and enables him to guarantee the height, width and placing of every piece of scenery.

256

Next in importance comes 'Document C', which contains the *twelve desirable measurements* that hold the secrets of the working of the stage.

Another document will convey to a business manager the capacity, financial and physical, of the house, and its amenities. But these documents do not come under the head of simple setting, they are to be set out in other connections and it will suffice if here a beginning is made towards the rationalization of the theatre by the study and adoption of 'Document A'. If there be any definite reasons against the contents of this form being made immediately a standard convention all over the country, there is at least none whatever against making the whole thing a standard *desideratum* throughout the country. Even if the forms were used and filled in, perforce incompletely, that in itself would crystallize our state at the present and be a constant pointer to the future, and though the materials themselves be still, as now, only half at hand, we could no longer plead blindness but should see what we *ought* to have.

And then, and not till then, shall we be in a position to turn and seek to increase our knowledge in three other directions; first, of the Science of Sight-lines, second, of Full-theatre Procedure (which will teach us among other things how to make backcloths and cycloramas), third, of the specialized craft of Scene-painting (from which we may learn how to design our painted details), and having mapped out these countries we may at last consider ourselves capable of taking no unimportant part in the theatre as a scarcely-to-be-reckoned figure, but, stepping beside its leaders, offer a new conception and a new life to the Art of Theatrical Presentation.

SPECIFICATION OF SETTING EQUIPMENT, *SO AND SO THEATRE*

CURTAINS, ETC.

Colour: *Warm putty.*

No. of 3 ft. strips: *4—7—4; also 4, 1' 6" strips.*

No. of borders: *1.*

Traverses: (*a*) *Back convertible.*
(*b*) *Additional traverse.*
May be hung at any depth.

Centre Backing: *18' × 20' sky-cloth.*

Spare Sets of Lines:
Front: *2 for front cloths.*
Back: *3.*

Extras: *Sides may be turned into wings.*

FURNITURE

Kitchen Suite: { *4 plain Windsor chairs.*
2 armed ,, ,,
1 table.

Living-room Suite: *1 settee, 2 armchairs, 2 occasional tables, 1 long table in 3 parts, round ends.*

Covers: (*a*) *1 set plain dark green.*
(*b*) *1 ,, cretonne (flowers on cream).*
(*c*) *1 ,, faded red (small pattern).*

Window Curtains: *3 sets to match covers.*
1 set plain deep cream.

Extras: *1 plain wooden hearth curb.*
1 divan 6' × 2' × 1' 6"
6 cushions with 2 sets covers to match (a) and (b) above.

DETAILS OF SCENERY

Doors,
  Single: *2, 3 ft.*
  Double: *1, 6 ft.*

Windows: *1 casement, 3 ft.*
      1 French, 6 ft.

Fireplaces: *1 ordinary.*

Backings,
  Door: *2 black double screens.*
  Fire: *1 ,, ,, screen.*

Rostrums: *4, 6' × 3' × 1' 6"*

Steps: *1, 2-tread, 6 ft. long.*
   2, ,, 3 ,, ,,

Braces & stage-screws: *12.*
     brace-weights.

Extras:

259

SPECIFICATION

LIGHTING

230 volts A.C.	CIRCUITS	WATTS PER LAMP	COLOURS IF FIXED	NO. OF LAMPS PER CIRCUIT
Pross batten	3	*100*	*Variable*	*5*
No. 2 batten		*None*		
Sky batten	3	*500*	*Variable*	*4*
Floats	3	*60*	*,,*	*5*
F.O.H. spots	3	*500*	*,,*	*1*
Dips	*2 a side*	*500*		*1*

DIMMERS	TYPE	LOAD	CIRCUIT
2	*wire*	*2000 w.*	*to plug into*
2	*,,*	*500 w.*	*any circuit.*
1	*liquid*	*8000 w.*	

Extras: *4 strips of 6, 60 w. lamps.*
      1 baby spot, 250 w.

Fig. 267. *Suggested specification-form for theatres using curtain sets.*

Bibliography

The following list of books and articles dealing especially with the simple side of setting may be useful to the reader. I have never devoted myself to discovering the whole literature on the subject and so these are only the titles of such books as I have come across in normal study of the subject. Some were eminently worth finding, some less so.

RODNEY BENNETT, M.A. *Let's do a Play.* (Nelson).

RODNEY BENNETT, M.A. *Play-production for Amateurs.* (Curwen.)

ERNEST F. DYER, B.A. *Producing School Plays.* (Nelson.)

W. G. FAY. *How to make a Simple Stage.* (French.)

W. G. FAY. *A Short Glossary of Theatrical Terms.* (French.)

ROY MITCHELL. *Shakespeare for Community Theatres.* (Dent, 1919.)

C. B. PURDOM. *Producing Plays.* (Dent.)

MARY RICHARDS. *Practical Play Production.* (Evans.)

MILTON SMITH. *The Book of Play Production for Little Theatres, Schools and Colleges.* (Appleton, 1926.)

MARJORIE SOMERSCALES. *The Improvised Stage.* (Pitman, 1932.)

WESTON WELLS. *A simple Fit-up Stage.* (British Drama League, 1926.)
    An article in *Drama* for Oct. 1926. Reprinted by the National Federation of Women's Institutes (illus.).

ANGUS WILSON. *The Small Stage and its Equipment.* (Allen & Unwin, 1930.)

ANGUS WILSON. *Scenic Equipment for the Small Stage.* (Allen & Unwin, 1930.)

ANGUS WILSON AND HAROLD RIDGE. *The Planning of the Stage.* (British Drama League, 1933.)
    1. In Small Halls.
    2. In Little Theatres.
    Articles in *Drama* for March and April, 1933 (illus.).

In Pitman's large 2-volume collection *Theatre and Stage* the following series of articles contain relevant matter: all are illustrated.
    F. E. Doran, *Aspects of Production.*
    C. de Reyes, *The Little Theatre and its Stage.*
    Hal D. Stewart, *Theory and Practice of Stagecraft.*
    Angus Wilson, *Home-made Scenic Equipment.*

Citizen House, Bath, have put out some pamphlets of typewritten sheets on *Planning Our Stage, A simple Collapsible Theatre for Village Halls* and *Scene and Property Making.*

Almost all metal parts and pieces of equipment mentioned in this book may be purchased from firms of theatrical hardware makers such as (in England) Hall Stage Equipment Ltd., Nona Works, Wynne Road, Brixton, London S.W. 9., and (in America) J. R. Clancy Inc., Syracuse, New York (whose catalogues make a veritable grammar of theatrical minutiae).

Extensions to Bibliography, 1937-1963

This was a simple enough bibliography in 1937, but almost a new world of reading is opened to the student of the subject since then.

First of all, while *Stage-Setting* was in the press Frank Napier's *Curtains for Stage-Setting* appeared, a first-class book from a practical man whose memory, as a colleague, I am glad to salute.

Next comes a regular 'bible' of the whole subject of setting on a large scale. It was published in Germany in 1929 but I did not see it here in England until the late '30s. It was Friedrich Kranich's *Bühnentechnik der Gegenwart* (Modern Stage Technique), 2 vols., Munich and Berlin, 1929 and 1933, with a total of 767 pages and 1106 illustrations— a tremendous work, and all in German, both language and thought.

Next came *Stage Scenery and Lighting* by Samuel Selden and Hunter D. Sellman, published first in America and then in England but without a date. This has run into later editions.

Scenery for the Theatre by Harold Burris-Meyer and Edward C. Cole was another American work (published in England in 1939) and was perhaps the first to deal with the construction of full scenery in close detail.

Traité de Scénographie by Pierre Sonrel (Paris 1943) gave a historical and modern account of continental technique, with an especially valuable section on scenic perspective.

Theatre Scenecraft by Vern Adix was published in America in 1956 and is a wide-ranging, general survey of the subject, containing useful chapters on scene paint.

Stage Scenery by A. S. Gillette (New York 1959) concerns itself in great detail with constructional methods and has many precise diagrams.

Between all these books the subject is now pretty well covered. The only reservation is that the bulk of information on the carpentry of flat-building comes from America where the technique is different from English technique. I made some attempt to redress the balance here in *The Oxford*

Companion to the Theatre (London 2nd ed., 1957) under the heading 'Flat', where a brief account of the English traditional method of building is given—and so far as I know the only printed account of this very special technique.

The subject of scene painting still awaits a major study. Frederick Lloyd's *Scene Painting* (as far back as about 1875) is still a valuable account. The serial articles by Henry L. Benwell in *Amateur Work* (vols. 4, 1st ed., and 5, 6, 7, 8, popular reissue, 1884 onwards) still have their interest, but are almost unavailable now. Vladimir Polunin studied *The Continental Method of Scene Painting* in 1927 (London). Emil Pirchan produced the very useful *Bühnenmalerei* in German (Vienna 1946). Harald Melvill gave a general account in *Designing and Painting Scenery* (London) in 1950. And Donald Oenslager edited some brief class-notes from the American scenepainter Bradford Ashworth (New Haven, Conn.) in 1952 which have some very valuable material.

Beyond these, several books though not dealing in any detail with the construction and handling of full scenery yet contain some references; such for example as Doris Zinkeisen's *Designing for the Stage* (London, Studio, n.d.) concentrating on design, and Percy Corry's *Stage Planning and Equipment* (London 1949) and *Planning the Stage* (London 1961) both dealing chiefly with technical equipment. To these should be added the second volume of *Traité d'aménagement des salles de spectacles* by Louis and Georges Leblanc (Paris 1950), the second volume of Werner and Gussman's *Theatergebäude* (Berlin 1954) dealing with modern German technique; and also the very useful Norwegian study *Vi rigger en scene!* (Oslo 1958).

For varieties of new styles of staging there is useful information in Walden P. Boyle's *Central and Flexible Staging* (Los Angeles 1956).

A Footnote to the 2nd Edition, 1964

The extended bibliography takes the reader from my simple stage settings into the heart of the complications of full scenery. What else is needed to bring him up-to-date before we part? Perhaps some reminder of the fact that all modern progress is not inevitably by way of greater technical complexity. Certainly one branch of the modern theatre sees its future not in a further development of full scenery but in a simplification into 'non-scenery', if I may use such a term, or into 'non-illusionist scenery'. But really this is no more than a reversion from *scenery* back to *stage setting*, as defined in this book.

I have been accused of 'overcompartmentalizing the types of setting'. I am unrepentant, for I find that my divisions have been useful to me. I am able as it is to take the 'Costume' setting, the 'Background' setting and the 'Symbol' setting, and the combination of these in the 'Detail' setting, and demonstrate that in them are contained all the great basic methods of scenic history up to the invention of perspective and full changeable scenery.

I am further able, after the experiments of recent years, to point out that any rebellion against the limitations of the proscenium arch—any attempt to 'abolish the proscenium'—must turn to one of these as the alternative (see *The Open Stage*).

All open-stage experiments must make use, however simple or however complicated, of the principles of 'Symbol' setting (a name which, I believe, covers exactly the same province as that which Glynne Wickham, in his second volume of *Early English Stages* (1962) has called 'emblem' settings). Any theatre-in-the-round production makes use of 'Symbol' setting in precisely the same way—whether its symbol be no more than a plain table or is an elaborate structure of skeleton walls and doors. This is as true of a modern play such as John Arden's *The Door* as produced in the round at the Studio I designed for the Drama Department of Bristol University as it is of a medieval play such as *The Castle of Perseverance* produced in the round, in the open air, near Lincoln (see my *The Medieval Theatre in the Round*, London 1957).

For the nature and design of the open stage itself on which the Symbol Setting is placed, the principles governing the Background Setting are fully applicable. A true open stage is no more than an organized Background Setting to suit any performance. It is particularized for a given performance by the use, to a larger or smaller extent, of the principles of Symbol Setting.

But beyond all this, the recent study of the Tudor Interludes has taught us how really simple, and yet really sufficient, a pure Background Setting can be. (It has done more: it has shown how a forgotten dramatic form exists which if 're-edified' (to use an old term) would offer a new field for modern playwrights—an opportunity for pungent, evocative dramatic entertainments on a wide variety of subjects but entirely free from the limitations of scenery, and capable of being presented in any sizeable room or hall with the barest minimum of essentials in the matter of setting, frequently not even requiring a stage). The early Interludes were generally played in halls, and often directly on the hall floor among the spectators and with the hall Screen as background. There were, as a rule, two doors in the Screen that afforded entrances. Between these might be set up a *traverse* of exactly the same nature as that shown in Fig. 7, p. 24 above (but not necessarily with the platform). Provision was thereby made for a system of presentation that could be flexible enough and expressive enough to stage almost any play in the great Elizabethan corpus of drama. The only two things lacking were a means of working flying figures and the opportunity for traps—and the latter of these is soon provided with the installment of a raised stage.

Indeed, the whole design of the mature Elizabethan public playhouse was (as far as our present knowledge goes) nothing more than a development of the arrangement just described. (See my *The Seven Ages of the Theatre* (1961) pp. 127-141 and 155-184.)

Finally and in a class of its own, there is the oldest setting style of all, the style that was sufficient for the drama of primitive ritual and for the presentation of the ancient mummers' plays and 'St. George' plays—that is, the dress and mask alone, in other words the 'Costume' setting, indispensable to all the styles, and still the most provocative, the most evocative and the least understood today of all our theatrical means.

There is no technical procedure in all the setting of the above great province of the theatre—historical or modern-experimental—which will extend the carpenter, who has a knowledge of the contents of this book, more than to the exciting use of his own ingenuity.

For readers, then, who seek wider information on more developed procedures in full scenery there is the amplified bibliography here to guide them. For readers who seek extension in the use of new methods there are the old techniques outlined in the book itself (and their adaptation if need be— and often there will be but little need), and the new world of possibilities for applying them.

Index

This index is intended to supply the place of a glossary by referring the reader to an illustration of, or an example of the use of, all the technical words employed in the book.

Such terms as are included in the index only for definition will not necessarily be given page references for every occasion of their use in the book, only for those which most clearly illustrate their meaning.

It may be useful, upon meeting a word in reading whose meaning is not familiar, to refer to the index to find its use in another context.

The only illustrations indexed are those which fall under the heads of 'exterior' or 'interior scenes'. All others are referred to in relevant passages of the text.

above
  in stage parlance, 62
Abraham Lincoln, 192, 195–
abstract built detail set, 170
acme fastener, 211
acting area, 17, 41, 50, 52, 77, 81, 125
  marked out for rehearsals, 193
actors
  effect on curtains, 136
  curtains' effect on, 195
  too exclusively regarded, 248
act wait
  place for heavy scene change, 192
'ang-kary' coupler, 89
apron stage, 234
Archer, William, 219
arch-piece, triple, 225, 227–, 239
arena flood lantern, 77
armed batten set, 142–, 245

arras set
  side-hung, 50–
  standing, 59, 64–
' artificial silk', 117
Arts League of Service, 83–

backcloth, small inset, 170, 185, 224, 239
background detail setting, 171–
background setting, 13, 14, 21–
backing, 138
  to centre back opening, 56
  to doors, 138, 202, 252
  to fireplaces, 182, 200, 216, 252
  to hire, 263
  to side entrances, 57
  to windows, 138, 202, 246
balcony, 70, 223, 241, 242
  Elizabethan, 162
ball, fibre
  for curtain track, 110
balustrade, 223, 228, 239, 243

batten
    = a length of wood, 84, 183, 228
    = a row of lamps, 125, 145, 255
    frame of, for curtain set, 121–
    in place of extension fittings, 39
    short, for wing curtains, 145
batten-out, to, 97, 183, 222, 228
Beggar's Opera, The, 152
below
    in stage parlance, 62
Bennett, Rodney, 82
block (*see also* pulley), 121, 123
bobbin, fibre
    for curtain track, 109
Bolton sheeting, 116, 117
border, 42, 77, 82, 86, 88, 121–, 129, 131, 144, 250
boy-students' stage, 55
brace, 42
    diagonal door, 210
    extending, 211, 252
    foot-brace, 215
    line-prop, 48, 235
    rough form of, 184
brace, cross-corner, 26, 28, 29, 30, 229
    externalized, 210
    obviated, 227
brace-foot, 211, 212
brace, French, 34, 35, 37, 215
braceweight, 34, 212, 252
    home-made, 213
bracing doors, 213
brail back, to, 49
bridle, 98, 124, 134
brown paper
    as profile stiffening, 183, 218
Burnet's, Messrs B., 119

cable grip, 44, 52
cable, wire, 43
casement cloth, 117
ceiling
    over curtain set, 145

centre back opening
    backing of, 56
    use for scenery, 49, 54, 129, 221, 245
centre line, 123
chain, bright
    for weighting curtain, 47
chesterfield suite, 253
claw hammer, 184
cleat, 123
columns
    of curtain strips, 224, 225
concrete braceweights, 213
conical winch
    for increasing purchase, 112
compensating strip
    in 3-fold hingeing, 30–
corrugated cardboard
    use in models, 193
costume setting, 15
Count Albany, 137
counterweight, 111
cowling of lights, 77
cup hook, 51
curtain
    on flat, 144
    on screen, 37, 39, 40
    representation on models, 193
    supporting heavy, 48
curtain, front
    etiquette of, 101–
    noisy and quiet, 109
    roller drop, 108
    simple drop, 101, 108
    'tabs', 58, 101
    timing of, 104, 205
    working of, 106–
    working of 'drapes', 86, 111
curtain hook, 47
curtains, rings on
    attached to webbing, 47
    for columns, 224
    for traverse, 132
curtain set
    atmosphere of, 138, 146, 195
    batten frame for, 121–
    ceiling on, 145

colour, 118
curved back in, 126
diagonal back in, 126
essential description of, 250
for flying, 142
hire of, 263
material, 116–
openings in, 137–
providing own proscenium, 82, 83, 86, 89
pulleys for, 121–
purist, 137–
supported from above, 121–, 142
supported from floor, 52, 64, 83, 87
supported from sides, 49, 51, 145
weave and lighting, 117
wing sides for, 85, 88, 126, 128, 145
curtain strips
actors disarranging, 136
as wings, 145
details in two adjacent, 199–
fulness, 130
half-width, 131, 181, 200, 201, 223, 224,
importance of not sewing, 119
on screens, 64
on screens for backing, 139
overlap of, 132, 177, 199–
removal for opening, 85, 138, 180
rolling of, 176, 178–
storing of, 117
use of short, 85, 137, 180
webbing band for, 130
curtain track, 87
system of best commercial, 110
curtain weighting, 47
curve
hanging curtains in, 126
cutcloth, 185
cut-out pieces, 228
cyclorama, 186, 202, 224, 247, 250

detail setting
compared with full setting, 22
compared with scenery, 155
definition, 15, 150–
distinct from permanent set, 152
examples of, 195–, 219–, 233–
proscenium necessary for, 75
special arrangement, 244–
varieties, 169–, 184–
details of scenery
behind windows, 138
distinct from full scenery, 150
essential stock of, 251
fitting curtain widths, 176, 201
in centre back opening, 54
in period scenes, 73
Lena Ashwell Players and, 141
on Elizabethan stage, 162
on Greek stage, 156
painted, 58, 170, 182–
plot of, 206
representational built, 170, 176, 182
simplified built, 186–
varieties, 169–
with folded screens, 74
with footed screens, 69–
diagonal back curtain, 126
dips, 255
documents, A, B and C, 256
doors
construction, 209–
direction of opening, 202–, 214
flimsy, 207
for curtain sets, 176, 209–
hingeing, 203–, 252
in A.L.S. steel fit-up, 85
in A.L.S. wooden fit-up, 88
in curtain sets, 180
not suitable with screens, 74
placing of, 199–
presetting, 224
sills, 208
upright bracing of, 214

double, to
  a backcloth, 226
  furniture, 73
  scenes, 221, 224
down-stage, 61
drapes
  fixing, 86
  overcoming weight of, 111, 112
  working of, 111
drawing pins for curtains, 178, 181
drawing room plays, 188, 253
drop, a, 101, 108

eight essential measurements, the, 256
Egypt
  simple framing in, 184
ekkuklema, 55
Elizabethan stage, 55, 159, 161, 162, 234
ensoflex, 95
equipment, minimum stage, 249–
exterior scenes illustrated
  arbour, fig. 99
  balcony, figs. 98, 262
  bridge, fig. 179
  camp, fig. 182
  cell, fig. 258
  cottage, fig. 203
  field, fig. 181
  garden, figs. 97, 173, 174, 176, 197
  mountains, fig. 240
  nativity, figs. 200, 201
  public square, fig. 257
  rampart, fig. 103
  river, figs. 198, 202
  seashore, fig. 195
  stile, fig. 199
  street, figs. 175, 260
externalization of braces, 210
eye bolt, 46

Fabrics Co-ordinating Committee
  Second report of, 119

Failures, The, 172
Father, The, 192
festivals, 208, 247, 248–
fire flicker, 217
fireplace,
  construction, 216
  in curtains, 181, 199, 200
  in footed screens, 71
fireproofing, 119
  and plywood, 222
fit-up
  guy-rope, 89
  steel tube, 87–
  wood, 82–
fit-up frame, 121–, 235
flat, 25, 27, 96
  as support of curtain, 144
  as wing, 245
  between curtains, 209, 246
  record of, in model, 193
  triple hingeing, 31
  two, as inset, 185
flies, 108, 115, 142
flipper, 37, 39
floats, 256
flood lantern, 76, 255
flying, 115, 142
F.O.H., 255, 256
foot-brace, 215
footlights, 256
foot scenery, to, 99
fourth wall, the, 81
frame detail, 171, 244, 246
frame up, to, 182
Fraser, Claud Lovat, 152
front scene, 71, 233
furniture
  home made, 254
  in models, 193
  loan stock of, 252

gate, property iron, 238
'giving' an exit, 204
glueing, 29
government silk, 116, 118
Greek stage, 54, 55, 155
Green Goddess, The, 219–

grip, cable, 44, 48, 52
groundrow, 56, 170, 185, 218, 224
grummet (or grommet), 98
guy rope, 48
guy rope curtain set, 52, 89

halve joint, 27, 28, 34, 216
hanging iron, 99
Hatter's Castle, 172
head block, 123
hessian, 117, 228
hingeing, 30–
   of rostrum, 230
   significance of door, 202–
hinge, kicking a, 35, 36
hinge
   loose butt, 37, 38, 227
   loose pin, 97, 216
   panorama, 143
   reversible pin, 38
   screen, 32–
Hippolytus, 137
hiring scenery, 193, 263

inessentials of scenery, 153, 157, 162, 164
inner stage, 55, 234
inset scene, 185, see fig. 197
insetting hinges, 30
interior scenes illustrated
   bedroom, figs. 180, 183, 263
   castle, fig. 196
   farm, fig. 215
   kitchen, fig. 104
   office, figs. 105, 213
   period, fig. 106
   rajah's palace, fig. 242
   room, figs. 42, 100, 178, 185, 186, 212, 214, 259, 261, 266
   staircase, fig. 178
   temple, fig. 101, 244
   theatre box, fig. 216
intervals
   effect on scene design, 192, 236–
   timing of, 102
iron gate, property, 238

Jacobean stage, 159
Japanese scenery, 186–
joints, 26–
Jones, Inigo, 72

kicking a hinge, 35, 36
kitchen plays, 253
Komisarjevsky, T., 172

left, stage-, 60
Lena Ashwell Players, 140, 175
lighting
   essential five points of, 254–
   of background sets, 76–
lines
   adjustment of curtain, 135
   long, short, and centre, 123
   untidy curtain, 59
   working, of tabs, 106
loan stock of scenery
   details in, 251
   travellers borrowing from, 248
long line, 123
loose covers, 253

magazine illustration
   analogy with setting, 154, 157
Malvaloca, 152
mask, to, 56, 82, 139, 163
masking
   tests of, 193, 194
   affair of theatre, 250
Master of the House, The, 105
material of curtains, 116–
maypole, 15, 23
mediaeval stage, 55
Middle Watch, The, 137
model
   use in design, 193
mortise and tenon, 26, 27, 91, 229

narrow curtain strips, 131, 181, 200, 201, 223
nativity, setting a 186

net, used in cut-outs, 228
Nicoll, Prof. Allardyce, 102, 155, 156
Nō plays, scenery in, 186–

offstage, 62
on-and-off-stage, 62
onstage, 62
openings, in curtain sets, 136–
  in pure curtains, 138
opposite-prompt side, 60
overlap
  of back curtains, 181, 202
  of curtain strips, 132, 177, 199
  of frame of battens, 122
  of front curtains, 86, 106, 107
  of sides on back, 200, 201
  of strips in traverse, 133
  of traverses, 133, 134
oxylene, 222

pack, scenery, 28
Padman, Miss May, 117, 213
painted detail, 58, 170, 182–, 246
period suggested by detail, 73
permanent set, 151, 152, 171
perspective
  influence on scenery, 163, 164
pin hinge, 97
  reversible, 38
plastered back wall, 122, 138, 251
plasticine, use in models, 193
plot
  of details, 206
  of movement, 72
  of scenery, 190–, 235
Pozzo, Andrea, 163
producer
  two sorts of, 191
  use of model to, 193
  views on Abraham Lincoln, 195
profile, 37, 183, 218
  tree in, 239
projected detail set, 247
prompt corner, 61

prompt side, 60
prop, line, 48
proscenium arch
  ancestor of, 54
  curved, 95
  derivation of, 55
  filling in above, 99
  in fourth wall, 82
  necessary for tabs, 59
  permanent, a, 92
  removable, a, 96
  simple, a, 91
proscenium wings, 244
proskenion, 55
pross batten, 255
pulleys
  double sheave block, 123
  position of, for curtain frame, 121–
  single sheave block, 123
purist curtain set
  backings, 139
  character, 146
  openings, 137, 138

rail, 26, 27, 28
  toggle, 97
railway, see curtain track
rake, 34, 61, 215
real detail set, 170
renaissance stage, 54, 161
representational built details, 170, 176, 182, 244, 252
  simplified, 186–
return
  as noun, 51, 53, 67
  as verb, tr., 50, 58
  as verb, intr., 39, 66
reveal, 94, 96, 210, 218
  loose pin hinges for, 97
reveal sill, 210
Ridge, C. Harold, 77, 256
right, stage-, 60
riser, a, 231
Rochdale Curtain Theatre set, 145
roller drop, 108

rolling curtain strips, 85, 177–, 218, 224, 225, 250
Romeo and Juliet, 233–
rostrum, 222, 223, 228, 239, 243
Rules for Management of Places of Entertainment, 116, 119
run a flat, to, 28, 144

safety pins for curtains, 178, 181
sandbag as braceweight, 34, 213
sandwich rolling rods, 179
scene change
  and intervals, 192
  behind traverse, 129, 233,234
  difficult in arras sets, 58
  doubling instead of, 221, 226
  in footed screens, 71
  in sight of audience, 71, 103
  of inset scenes, 186
  presetting for, 224
  scene waits, 220, 224
scene-plot, 190–, 235
scenery
  and realism, 160, 163
  definition of, 149–
  Elizabethan, 55
  'full' and 'detail', 150,155,157
  inessentials of, 153, 157
  in Japanese Nō plays, 186
  origins, 15, 54, 156
  rise of, 159–
scene store, 192, 263
scenic contractors, 263
screen
  as a detail, 173
  as background detail, 172, 246
  as background setting, 23–, 39, 41
  as backing, 56
  folded, 74, 224, 226, 240, 241, 242
  footed, 64–
screw-eye, 84, 123, 211, 215, 252

set piece, 69, 170, 185, 222
  simple construction for, 182
shackle, 45
sheave
  single and double, 123
short line, 123
sideboard-cupboard, 217, 224
side entrances
  in curtains, 57
  ways of backing, 57, 58
side-hanging, 42
side-hung sets, 49, 50–, 145
sight-lines, 57, 256, 257
sill-iron, 208, 209, 227
  reveal sill, 210
Simonson, Lee, 172
simple setting, definition, 22
skeleton detail set, 173
skene, 55
skirting boards
  for walls, 173
  on screens, 73
sky, 122, 247
sky batten, 255
sky sheet or cloth, 84, 138, 186, 202, 218, 224, 250, 251, 263
Sladen-Smith, F, 134
snap hook (*see also* spring hook), 47
Somerscales, Marjorie, 74
specification form of setting equipment, 249–
spot lantern, 76, 255
spring hook or snap hook, 51, 133, 143
stage directions, 60–
stage screw, or hand screw, 84, 212, 252
stage setting
  and table setting, 160
  definition, 149–151
staircase, 228
standing arras set, 59, 64
standing piece, 223
standing scene, 152
staple, 106, 133
steps, 222, 223, 231

stile, 26, 27
strike, to, 144, 186, 223, 234
strolling players' stage, 55
support
  methods of scene, 42
  of doors and windows, 85, 88
  of proscenium, 92, 98
  with braces, 34, 211–
swivel batten for wing curtains,
  85, 88, 126, 128
symbol setting, 15, 187

table, extending, 206, 254
tabs (*see also* front curtain), 58,
  101
tape for windows, 216
Tempest, The, 55
Thersytes, 16
thickness-piece, *see also* reveal,
  94, 218
thimble, 45
Thirteenth Chair, The, 137
Thompson, Woodman, 152
three by one, 25
three stage theory, the modern,
  234
timing of front curtain, 104–
toggle rail, 97
top-hanging, 42
  beams to allow, 92
  for full set, 122–
top-joining, 129
topping, or adding top extensions, 38, 39
travelling scenery
  and borrowing, 248
  hingeing for, 31
  painting for, 182
traverse
  back curtain on rings, 87
  for detail sets, 246, 250
  for narrowing sets, 241
  in Elizabethan plays, 233–
  made of top-joined strips,
    129–, 132–
  on a single wire, 134
  side-hung, 134, 146

tread, a, 231
trick-lines, 210, 215
tubing, steel, as element of sets,
  52
  coupler for, 89
  fit-up, 87
  for curtain track, 109
twelve desirable measurements,
  the, 257
tyers, 144
tying tapes, 131

Unnamed society, the, 134
up-and-down-stage, 62
upstage, 61

velvet, 116
  chenille, 117
verse speaking, slow, 233

weave, of curtains relative to
  light, 117
webbing curtain band, 47, 130
Wells, H. Weston, 75
whipping a rope end, 44–
winch, for front curtains, 112
window
  bay, 216
  in A.L.S. steel fit-up, 88
  in A.L.S. wooden fit-up, 85
  in footed screens, 71
  in pure curtain sets, 137, 138
  long, 216
  panes, 216
  sash, 215
  simply represented, 243
Windsor chair, 253
wing
  = a part of a setting, 83, 126,
    128, 144, 145, 244
  = wing-space, 50, 58, 132
wire strainer, 43, 52
woollen fabric for curtains, 116,
  117